WATER UNDER THE BRIDGE

WATER UNDER THE BRIDGE

LOADS OF OTHER STUFF TOO

BY DON BARRY

A JOURNEY INTO VALUES-SHAPED LEADERSHIP

Water Under the Bridge
Published by Don Barry
New Zealand

ISBN 978-0-473-30338-9 (Softcover)
ISBN 978-0-473-30339-6 (ePUB)
ISBN 978-0-473-30340-2 (Kindle)

Third printing

Editing & Production:
Andrew Killick
Castle Publishing Services
www.castlepublishing.co.nz

Cover Design & Illustration:
Angela Keoghan
The Picture Garden
www.thepicturegarden.co.nz

Author Photo:
Ruth Gilmour
www.ruthgilmourphotographer.co.nz

See the notes section of this book
for Bible usage and other permissions.

Dedication

When I told Karen, my wife of 41 years, that I planned to dedicate this book to her, she looked at me and with the hint of a twinkle in her eyes said, 'I'd rather have clothes.'

Classic! So Karen – funny, practical, honest and with a smidgeon of playful provocation.

This is for you Karen. I've loved the journey we have taken together. I couldn't have done it without you and am grateful beyond words for your constant love and your unflinching support; as for the clothes, let's see how the book sells.

Contents

Introduction

This book has been over 36 years in the making. It started in 1977 when my wife Karen and I began working in full-time ministry.

Over the years, we experienced a lot, and learnt a bit. Some of the lessons were written in 'blood' (ours) long before they were written in printer's ink. There have been times in our journey when I wished I had some kind of map that could explain the contours of the places I found myself lost in. I longed for someone to explain the reasons and meaning behind the pain I felt, and put things into some kind of context. I wanted to find hope in my struggle.

My prayer is that this humble effort to explain our journey might provide just such a map and encouragement for some other perplexed travellers on their faith journey.

This book is unavoidably autobiographical.

Frederick Buechner, a master of the written word and one of my favourite authors, comments that writing autobiography,

> feels a bit like showing your baby pictures to a complete stranger. It also has a hint of being a bit geriatric. Here is an old codger attempting to put his affairs in order, marking his cherished possessions so that his descendants won't bicker over them after he has passed; writing names on the backs of his photographs so that someday, somebody will be able to identify who these people were, if anybody should even be interested.[1]

While I am unapologetic about this book's autobiographical nature, I am very aware that any kind of autobiography has its perils. There are powerful temptations towards self-deception and hypocrisy as we tell our own stories. It is hard to see the truth; it is also hard to tell the truth. There is always the temptation to tell the story in a self-justifying manner that subtly, or perhaps not all that subtly, slants it in a way that places the storyteller in the best possible light. I offer this autobiographical work with the awareness that I am not exempt from these tendencies and temptations.

I didn't write the book thinking people would be captivated by the story, as much as I wrote hoping they would recognise principles and patterns that seemed to emerge and re-emerge in my life and the lives of other would-be leaders in both biblical and post-biblical times.

Hebrews 13:8 is a scripture that we love to quote, 'Jesus Christ the same yesterday and today, and forever.' The context, though, is important.

The previous verse states, 'Remember them which have the

rule over you, who have spoken unto you the word of God: whose faith follow, considering the end of their conversation' (KJV). This is an exhortation to look carefully at the lives of leaders who have been faithful, and to follow in their footsteps. Then the famous verse follows, 'Jesus Christ the same yesterday and today, and forever.' The two are connected in context as well as in sequence.

I think these verses are seeking to inform us that the principles and patterns God uses in developing leaders are somewhat constant, though the specifics always vary. God doesn't turn out leaders like chocolate soldiers, but He does allow His people to face common trials and familiar tests. We each have our unique story, but we cover common ground in our journeys.

It is for this reason that I dare to be so blatantly autobiographical. I believe that God intends that we will learn from one another. My story isn't just *my* story. Buechner puts the point sublimely, as always, 'If you can tell your own story with sufficient candour and concreteness, it will be an interesting story and in some senses a *universal story*'[2] (emphasis added).

I agonised over the issue of candour, not because I was unwilling to tell the whole story, but because there are parts of it that don't reflect well on certain situations and some characteristics I have observed in church leadership. I wondered if it would be better to be deliberately vague, so that I didn't give more cause for people to disrespect leaders in a culture that is already suspicious of those who dare to lift their heads above the herd.

I thought of David's song following Saul's demise, 'Tell it not in Gath, publish it not in the streets of Askelon; lest the daughters of the Philistines rejoice, lest the daughters of the uncircumcised triumph' (2 Samuel 1:20 KJV). Perhaps it would be best to simply bury the evidence, grit one's teeth and present the best picture possible for the sake of the greater good. I have no interest in muck-raking or scandal.

Just when I had settled on the idea that it would be best to leave out the more 'unsavoury' parts of the story, I thought of the well worn adage, 'If we don't learn from history we are bound to repeat it.' Was this a call to truth? Perhaps if I blew the whistle we could somehow prevent the same old damaging games from being replayed time and again with different players. And it seemed to me, upon reflection, that the lessons gleaned through difficulty would be much less meaningful if I failed to describe the ground from which they sprang.

I was nervous and wanted my motives to be right. I did a lot of soul-searching. I didn't want the unwelcome surprise of offending more people than I might possibly help, and I definitely didn't want the surprise of an angry lawsuit.

In the end, after turning the computer off and on innumerable times in indecision, I tried as best as I was able to plot a middle course. For some I will have told too much – I know I run the risk of offence. For others, particularly those who were part of the story, or at least recognise it, I will have failed to be bold enough.

I will tell the story with what I hope will be sufficient candour and concreteness, trusting that it will be, as Buechner suggested, interesting and universal – that you will see your story through the pages of mine and, in so doing, will perceive something of a 'map' that might provide some spiritual bearings and hope for your journey.

Don Barry
Hamilton
New Zealand

CHAPTER 1

Gathering Clouds

The 34 years since have bleached my memory of details; I can't remember the day or month; I don't recall the time of day, what he, or I for that matter, was wearing. I don't recall him knocking on my office door – he may have done, but that wouldn't have been in keeping with his usual style. What I do remember with vivid detail are the words he spoke and the steely glint in his eyes, 'Don, I feel one of us should leave, and I feel called to stay!'

I laughed nervously, 'That narrows my options somewhat doesn't it?'

'Yes it does,' he said, pleased with the way he'd got his message across. Then he turned and walked out. The delivery seemed well-rehearsed. He had clearly given not a little thought to how I should be moved on from what had become an untenable situation for us both.

In fact, I was later to hear him advise other ministers on how to get rid of a recalcitrant member of staff, and he suggested the exact same formula as a fail-safe method.

That short, characteristically curt conversation, brought the curtain down on my first experience of full-time church ministry.

It had started with much anticipation and promise some seven years earlier.

In the early 1970s Karen and I were caught up in our romance, courtship and subsequent marriage, and captured by the Charismatic Movement which, tsunami-like, swept through denominations of all kinds. We were Catholics – I had been a teenage convert and Karen came from a long line of Irish believers. Not long after entering into an experience of Holy Spirit empowerment, which we called the Baptism in the Holy Spirit, Karen and I started attending other churches that openly taught Charismatic truths.

We loved the excitement of that season – conferences, summer schools and visits to churches that we knew were on 'the cutting edge' – whatever that was supposed to mean. We certainly didn't understand what a 'cutting edge church' was, and I'm reasonably certain that the people who used the phrase to attract us to these churches had little more idea than we did. Among the gaggle of churches we visited in those days, we attended a Pentecostal church in a city near our hometown. It was lively and growing, and became a regular Sunday night feature in our Charismatic smorgasbord. There were a number of people coming from our hometown to this city church, so discussion soon developed about the possibility of a church plant.

Sure enough, it began in 1973 with a home-group, which 17 people attended on the inaugural night.

Full church life – as full as any church plant can be – followed soon after, and thus commenced the journey that was to end so decisively seven years later.

The man who led the church plant – I'll call him Dave – was an evangelist by gifting, and was never happier or more fulfilled than when preaching to a crowd scattered with unbelievers. His preaching was usually a mix of Bible passages, daily news and humour – and yet with remarkable regularity people surrendered to Christ and joined our flourishing little fellowship.

I was a school teacher and so sought to balance the demands of my job with the ever-increasing call to 'dedication', 'commitment' and 'radical discipleship' – by which we meant total involvement in church life.

For the most part, at least at the beginning, I didn't question this call to dedication. There seemed to be a convincing number of scriptures that pointed to the need for total commitment to Christ and to what Dave often referred to as the 'vision of the house'. Around this time, the Discipleship Movement rose to prominence. Led by a group of men based in Fort Lauderdale, Florida, this teaching of submission and loyalty to one's leaders went out into far-flung regions of the world.

I suspect, as is so often the case, that the Floridians had discovered principles that, in the right context and spirit, could and would be a blessing. But by the time these teachings reached places like New Zealand, they were shared among people who had no idea where Fort Lauderdale was and even less idea of the original intent of the message. Removed from their original context and spirit, the principles of the

Discipleship Movement ended up being used as rods and goads to exercise control and dominate people in ways that were unhealthy and far from godly. That, unfortunately, was our experience.

The voice calling us to deeper 'commitment' – which was measured in time, energy and money given to the church – became more and more strident and demanding.

Although I was beginning to have misgivings about some of the directions we were being taken, and about the methods being used to get us there, my reserve was relatively easily pressed into submission. All it took were some well-placed scriptures about giving up your life for the gospel. If those verses failed to silence the nagging questions, then there was always the coup de grace scripture, 'Touch not the Lord's anointed,' which would serve to silence any dissenting or vaguely critical comment or thought that ran contrary to the word of the senior pastor.

The obvious blessing of the Lord on the life of the fellowship seemed to be a strong indicator that what was happening was pleasing to God. Any uneasy thoughts concerning the church's direction, it seemed, must be misguided and inappropriate. We grew quickly in numbers and at times experienced seasons of Holy Spirit visitation during which remarkable things occurred. In one six-week period, over 60 people surrendered to Christ and some miraculous healings took place.

With the church now running at 70 to 90 people at any given Sunday service, Dave approached me and asked how I would feel about joining the full-time staff. I had already been functioning in an eldership role and it seemed a natural and, for the most part, desirable step towards a future in Christian ministry.

In 1977 I left my teaching job and joined the church staff.

My role initially consisted of a potpourri of tasks – from maintenance on our newly purchased building, running the crèche on ladies' mornings, running a children's midweek programme and visitation, to occasionally preparing messages for Sunday teaching slots.

I loved Bible study and, perhaps through a mix of training and spiritual giftedness, teaching seemed to naturally flow from me.

In so many respects, Dave and I could have – and perhaps should have – complemented each other brilliantly and made an effective team. He was strong in evangelism, and bold in faith and the operation of spiritual gifts, while I was stronger in teaching and pastoral care.

In my naivety I certainly imagined it developing along those lines, but that was not to be.

The first hints of the stony road ahead came after a morning service in which I had delivered the main message.

Unbeknownst to me, someone had approached Dave after the service and complimented my preaching, 'That young man has a gift. He's a really good teacher.' I arrived at work the next morning and started my usual Monday morning assignment – running off cassette tapes of the previous day's messages for any who wished to rehear it or for people who had been unable to attend the services.

I was tucked up in the large cupboard that served as our tape library, copying cassettes, when I heard a rustle from the doorway behind me. I turned and there was Dave, leaning against the doorpost watching me with an obvious degree of intensity that I immediately found somewhat intimidating.

My cheerful greeting was met with a seemingly reluctant nod and a raising of the eyebrows. He remained motionless against the door frame, the uncomfortable silence and concentrated gaze stretching out for what seemed like a prolonged time.

Finally he broke the silence, 'Don, I'm a better teacher than you are.' There was a determined force to the words that seemed to match his physical posture. Then he quickly turned and strode into his office, firmly shutting the door behind him.

I was left utterly confused. 'What in heaven's name was that about?' I wondered.

Not having been party to the compliment that had been paid to my preaching the previous day, Dave's declaration had hit me like a drone attack. It seemed to be completely free of context and out of the blue.

Before I had time to process or properly reflect on what had occurred, the next missile was fired.

The following evening we had a training night at the church – a Timothy Class, we called it. Most of the church was present.

Before starting the scheduled teaching, Dave addressed those present, in a very serious manner,

'I have something important to say that I want you all to listen to and understand,' he started.

We all leaned forward in anticipation, wondering what subject would merit such gravity from our pastor.

'Don is not the teacher in this church – I am. Do you

understand?' Pointing in my direction he continued, 'He is not the teacher here – I am!'

With the point made, in a matter-of-fact way he turned and proceeded, apparently unfazed, to teach the evening's lesson.

The fact that I don't recall anything else that was said that evening isn't just a consequence of the intervening years. Though I sat through the remainder of the meeting, outwardly unmoved by Dave's vehement remarks, inwardly I was in turmoil.

I had never, to that point in my life, encountered anything like this degree of adamant defensiveness directed against me. I was confused. Why could the church not have more than one teacher? I had no interest in usurping Dave. Why was the acknowledgement of my gifting such a cause for concern? Dave's edicts were, in hindsight, indicative of powerful insecurity, but I didn't recognise it or understand it.

In the following days and weeks I did my best to forget what had happened. I kept my head low and tried to stay out of trouble. Dave announced to me that he felt led by God to be the 'only voice' in the church for a season. It was 12 months before I preached again.

We were part of a network of churches and met regularly in warm fellowship with the ministers of those congregations. Out of the relationships that were formed, I received several invitations to speak at other churches.

The first time an invitation came, I excitedly took it to Dave and asked if I could be allowed to forego a Sunday service at our church so I could speak at theirs.

Dave's response to that first invitation became the template for most of the subsequent occasions. I quickly learnt that they weren't worth the angst they caused. Dave perused the letter I had handed him, screwed it up and placed it in his rubbish bin. He then looked up and said, 'No I don't want you to go. I need you here that day.'

I returned, somewhat disappointed, to my office, trying to think why I would be so needed at our church on that particular Sunday.

Shortly afterwards my door pushed open and Dave entered, his face flushed with obvious anger. 'They don't need you,' he said pointing at me as I sat behind the inadequate shield that was my desk. 'They don't need you to soft-soap them with your so-called teaching! They need *me* to tell them the truth!'

With that he spun on his heels and left, slamming the door behind him.

As I think back on these times with the benefit of hindsight – and hopefully accumulated years of wisdom – I often wonder why I didn't just pack my few books and walk away. The writing was on the wall, even at that early stage. To this day I have never been able to adequately answer that question. Was it the strength of the *Call* I felt to full-time ministry? Was it the fear of the upheaval such a decision would cause between Dave and me, and in the life of the church? Was it the anxiety of having my small family, since Karen had given birth to our first child in the midst of the unfolding drama, being left without financial support? Perhaps it was a mix of all of these factors – holy and unholy, noble and ignoble. Anyway, the end result was that I remained.

There were seasons when Dave's insecurity would seem to

pass and the relationship between us was somewhat normal. Even in these relatively calm periods his drive for success (read 'church growth'), and what he assumed would be the resultant notoriety, were quite frightening.

He was, at heart, a pragmatist and was prepared to take whatever steps were required to achieve his goals.

Jon Krakauer wrote a book entitled *Into Thin Air*.[1] It's the true story of an ill-fated Everest expedition in May 1996. Krakauer writes of a phenomenon called 'summit fever'. This occurs when climbers become so obsessed with reaching the summit that they start making decisions that compromise the basic safety procedures that are so vital for effective climbing.

Apparently a similar obsession can grip fighter pilots. They become so focussed on their intended target that they ignore the warnings of the aircraft's instrument panel. They call it 'target fever'.

In the same way, hunters refer to 'buck fever'. In the excitement of a possible kill, the hunter doesn't properly identify their prey. Every hunting season, hunters and hikers are shot dead by 'fevered' marksmen.

I am convinced that there is a pastoral equivalent of summit fever, target fever and buck fever. I have never taken the time to name the phenomenon – perhaps 'revival fever' or 'church growth fever' could be contenders for an appropriate term. I have, however, seen and experienced its symptoms.

It causes basic values, usually considered sacrosanct and

inviolate, to be set aside. In the headlong rush for the summit of church 'success', people are *used* instead of *served*, and ethics are sacrificed to gain victory.

As C S Lewis once famously commented, 'We have shouted the name of Christ and enacted the service of Molech.'[2] In our church, at that time, we did this with frightening regularity.

This ailment, a kind of theological utilitarianism, caused us to shape our theology to match our aims, and led us into ethically murky territory.

One day, Dave strolled into my office to ask if I had filled in a report form for a Christian film that we had shown at church. The form governed the amount of royalty fees we would pay for public screening. I replied that I had, and he asked, 'Did you say that we previewed the film?'

'Yes,' I responded.

'Don't do that in future.'

Surprised and somewhat confused, I replied, 'But we did preview it. The form asked, did you preview the film? I ticked the yes box.'

Angered by my obvious sluggishness in understanding his drift, he spelled it out more clearly,

'If you tick that box we have to pay more; don't do it.'

My back stiffened and I found myself asking him,

'So you want me to lie?'

'Yes,' he replied without any obvious hesitation.

'I think you had better fill out any subsequent forms yourself. I'm not lying for you or anyone else,' I said, trying to contain and disguise a bubbling sense of outrage.

Once again the door slammed as he exited and I had the

sense that my response would somehow be added to a growing list of incidents which, at best, would highlight that I was not in sync with Dave's vision for the church and, at worst, would indicate that I was undermining the 'Lord's anointed'. I sighed, sat for a moment and then tried to get on with my day's work.

CHAPTER 2

The Storm Breaks

As time passed, the teachings of the Discipleship Movement, in our situation at least, became more assertive. Pastoral approval was increasingly required for decisions that would usually be left to a person's own discretion. For example, we would never consider buying a house or car without pastoral counsel and permission. You would never have considered dating, let alone marriage, without pastoral vetting and approval.

On one occasion Dave told me he was considering making it mandatory for people in the church to write and ask for permission to take holidays. His reasoning was that he could then space out people's absences so the church wouldn't have its usual drop in attendance during holiday periods.

Somehow, I have no recollection how, I managed to talk him out of that idea. But the ideas kept coming and I found myself often cast in the role of devil's advocate.

At some point, 'ideas' morphed into 'revelations'. This shift in the way suggestions and plans were communicated made dissent all the more difficult. It was one thing to raise doubts regarding Dave's ideas; quite another matter to challenge 'divine unveilings.'

Meanwhile, Karen and I were growing increasingly uncomfortable with the situation, and I felt I needed to make a stand. God had spoken to me on one occasion through a dream and a scriptural passage. Both conveyed the same message, and it wasn't easy to hear. I was a leader and God expected that I would do my level best to protect the flock and warn of impending trouble. The scripture that impacted me was Isaiah 56:10.

> For Israel's watchmen are blind, the whole lot of them. They have no idea what's going on. They're dogs without sense enough to bark, lazy dogs, dreaming in the sun… (MSG)

'Dumb dogs,' was how the KJV phrased it, which was a sobering thought. Was I like that? I felt convicted that on far too many occasions I had opted for safety and quiet rather than making my thoughts known regarding a course of action that I felt was ill-conceived or plain wrong.

I remember muttering something to the Lord about the fact that barking dogs tended to end up with a bullet through their heads. He didn't respond in words, but the silence seemed to convey something along the lines of, 'And your point is? You chose to accept the role of leadership and I expect you to act responsibly in it.'

To be honest, my barks from that point on were still pretty few and far between, by virtue of the fear of that final bullet, and when I did bark I'm sure it registered, in heaven at least, more like a Chihuahua than an Alsatian.

Dave came into my office one afternoon and announced

that God have given him a revelation. I shivered internally, and braced myself for what this newest revelation might mean.

I tried to appear calm, and asked what it was that he thought God had said. With a look of confident assurance, he announced that he thought God had shown him that the people in his congregation couldn't hear the voice of God unless they heard it through him as the senior pastor.

My immediate indignation emerged in the form of a question.

'Have you heard of the Reformation?' I asked incredulously.

'Of course I have,' he shot back, 'what on earth has that got to do with anything?'

I drew a deep breath and then explained what I had thought would be the obvious link.

'In the Reformation one of the basic truths that God restored to the church through Luther and his fellow reformers was that God didn't need a priesthood to mediate His presence, purpose and power to His people. It was *sola fide*, by faith alone. People can have a relationship with God that isn't dependent on others to mediate it to them.'

I waited for that to sink in, watching Dave closely for some hint of how my challenge was being perceived.

He simply dismissed me with a shrug, headed for the door and, in what seemed like an action replay of so many other occasions, said, 'I know what God spoke to me.'

My next move was probably unwise. Perhaps it was that I knew the bullet was coming sooner or later anyway and I thought now was as good a time as any; and this was an issue more important than most to take it for.

'I was better off as a Catholic,' I called out to the retreating figure.

He re-entered the door with a stunned look on his face.

'You were what?' he asked with a furrowed brow and an intense stare as if daring me to repeat what he thought I had just said.

'I was better off as a Catholic,' I repeated, perhaps more weakly than before, but still strongly enough to make the anger blaze in his eyes.

'Would you like to explain yourself?' he fumed.

'Sure,' I responded, imagining that I could hear a cartridge being placed into the loading mechanism of a rifle.

'When I was a Catholic we had an infallible pope but he lived in Rome 10,000 miles away and he never bothered me. Now I have a 'Pentecostal Pope' in the next office. This is untenable. You're taking us back into the Dark Ages!'

To my surprise, it was now I who was fuming, standing with fists clenched and placed in front of me on the desk, almost daring him to respond. Whether it was out of fear for what he might do in retaliation, or surprise at what he thought I might do, without any further words he simply turned and left my office.

I remained standing for a time, my heart beating faster and more violently than I had ever felt it beat before.

I looked out the window onto an old garage, where numerous wrecked cars were rusting into the ground, and couldn't help feeling the scene was strangely, ominously prophetic. A train wreck, as they say, was approaching at speed.

Around that time, a friend of mine named Mark called in to visit. He had previously been a member of our church, but had managed to 'escape' (I jest, but only mildly). He was on his way to a youth conference. While we drank tea, Mark asked Karen and me how we were managing.

The whole sorry story and our accompanying unhappiness poured out. Mark asked if he could mention our situation to the guest speaker at the conference and ask his advice.

To be truthful, I really didn't care what the man might say, but I was concerned that Mark didn't use our names or mention our geographic location. The last thing I needed was for news of our discontent to travel and get back to Dave.

Several days later, on his return journey, Mark called in to our home again.

'I asked the speaker about your situation,' he said.

'Yeah, what did he say?' I responded, my interest somewhat piqued.

'He asked how long you'd served here. I told him seven years. Then he told me to tell you: "Jacob served Laban seven years for Rachel. It's time to get out."'

The thought registered but I think I filed it in the later-to-be-considered basket. It was overshadowed in the short-term by an impending holiday Karen and I had planned.

We set out the next day on our much-needed break, with hearts heavier than our entire luggage combined. But the further we drove from the town's outer limits the better and lighter I felt. It was nice to have some time away from the imminent storm that was brewing.

With our two young children in tow (Karen had given birth to our beautiful daughter in 1978), we visited friends in various places and stayed at the coast, enjoying the sun, sand and watching the kids play.

As our 10 days away came to an end, a black, foreboding cloud seemed to grow as the distance to our town diminished.

Unplanned, we delayed the inevitable return home by calling again on a family we had stayed with at the beginning of the holiday. As we sipped our tea, I noticed our hosts having a conversation with their eyes, as only those long married can do.

'We think we had better tell you something that happened after you left here last week,' Peter said hesitantly.

With a sense of rising – but completely unspecific – dread, I quizzed him,

'What happened? What are you talking about?'

'Dave rang and interrogated us about your activities and the conversations you'd had with us. He said you are part of a coup attempt. He said that you are trying to take over his church.'

My emotions surfaced quickly and were as uncontrollable as a flooded stream that has broken its levee – incredulity, anger, outrage and, to my shame, not a few thoughts of violence.

We bade our friends goodbye and I determined that the sun would not set on my anger. It wasn't that I planned to deal with the situation in any kind of godly, scriptural manner; instead I decided that I would go back to have it out once and for all with Dave. In my mind I ran through the likely scenario, letting my imagination run free. I would challenge him and he, in true Dave style, would rise and defend his position by attacking me. At that point in my imaginings, I would strike out. I wasn't sure whether I'd lead with a right or left, or perhaps even a kick. It didn't really matter what I started with, I knew exactly how I wanted it to end – with Dave in his place and in no doubt about the fact that he had my resignation.

On the journey southwards, I enlightened Karen about my plans (minus the left and right – there was no need to worry her unduly). I saw her face light up when I mentioned the word 'resignation'. To this point in the story, I haven't focused on the damage Karen sustained during this unhappy saga. The effects were significant, and they had strained our marriage. At church, women were constantly being put down, as a natural corollary of the submission teaching. Karen had been left feeling like a member of some kind of sub-human species that could only have meaning if 'rightly related' (read 'subservient') to a male in particular, and males in general. The thought that perhaps a fresh start was possible brought a sense of relief to us both.

On arrival at our town, I dropped Karen home and drove straight to the church. I parked the car and strode into the office. My sister, who was the church secretary, saw the fiery determination in my eyes and, without a word, simply pointed to Dave's office.

There was a perverse sense of enjoyment in it being my turn to barge into *his* office without knocking.

He was completely thrown by my presence and unexpected arrival.

'Don, what are you doing back?' he stammered. 'You're supposed to be on holiday.'

'I'm back because I'm sick to death of a paranoid pastor chasing me around on holiday checking up on my movements and conversations and making pathetic and demented accusations about attempted coups!'

He rose from his chair and I remember clenching my fists and thinking, 'So far so good; right on cue.'

'Hang on just one minute,' he began to protest.

'Shut up and listen to me,' I demanded, and to my surprise he sat down meekly as I proceeded to unload seven years of pent-up frustration. There were a couple of moments when he made to register a differing opinion, but each time he was met with a firm, 'Shut up and listen.' Somewhere around the ten-minute mark, I realised with a start that we had departed from my imagined script. I was sure my right or left should have come into play by now.

Even the previously imagined headlines in the local paper, 'Pastor and Assistant in Brawl at Church,' hadn't deterred my determination to work the matter out one way or another.

What had happened instead was that, almost imperceptibly, Dave had grown quieter and quieter, and more and more pale. Finally his head slumped down and he rested it on folded arms atop his desk.

Then he began to weep. The weeping turned into a wail, and for 15 minutes an internal geyser opened up and played with a force that quietened and frightened me. I stopped talking and sat down.

By the time he had finished, I had too. We both sat exhausted, like a pair of battered prize-fighters – in the presence of each other, but more so in the presence of our own open wounds.

'Please don't leave me,' he begged. 'Don't resign. I'm having a nervous breakdown. All you have said is true. I need your help to turn this around.'

I was at a complete loss as to how to respond. This scenario was entirely off-script.

The best I could do was to weakly suggest that I would need to think about it and, utterly drained, I stood and left the office and headed for home.

In spite of some serious misgivings, Karen and I agreed that we must do our best for Dave and the congregation.

There had been many times over those seven years when I had read through the story of David and Saul. I guess I had always seen myself as David-like – the victim of a rampaging, envious, insecure king. I was very aware that Dave saw the same story from a different perspective, and in his casting of the tale he wasn't Saul but David – and I wasn't David, but Absalom.

Who knows the truth of it? I'd like to think my version was closer to reality than his, but I was keenly aware, even then, of the actions and attitudes within me that were probably – truth be known – more like Absalom than David.

I would read about David sparing Saul's life when it was easily within his reach to extinguish it. Saul would respond with gratitude and a promise never to hunt David again. Then you'd turn the page, and there was Saul, once again creeping up on David with a javelin in hand.

I always used to wonder what happened in Saul's experience to change his apparent contrition into a renewed and determined desire to kill David. Now I think I know. The answer is 'three months'.

It sounds like a strange, somewhat incongruous conclusion, but I suspect that the contrition Saul experienced in those cathartic moments was not of sufficient strength or duration to straighten the twisting that had been occurring in him for years.

Just a few months later, the old thoughts gained ascendency once again and the dark, paranoid imaginings took hold as before. This reminds me of J R R Tolkein's observation in *Lord of the Rings*, 'Always after a defeat and a respite, the Shadow takes another shape and grows again.'[1]

Meanwhile, back in the twentieth century, after a time of seeming tenderness, Dave's attitudes began to subtly revert back to older patterns. He began to refer to our fateful confrontation as 'that business,' and within weeks the conversation with which I began Chapter One had taken place. I had been dismissed.

A hurried and rather shallow church farewell was held and Karen and I found ourselves ostracised from those who remained in the fellowship. Several people made an attempt to say what we had meant to them. Some, in a rather cloak-and-dagger manner, said they would like to have known us better, but that it simply wasn't worth the wrath that they knew would come down on them.

Now we were adrift, and looking for our next harbour.

CHAPTER 3

'What was that all about?'

Karen and I had a lot of thinking to do. We considered a number of options for our future, including overseas study. In the midst of our deliberations, a member of the Executive of our denomination phoned to tell us about a church that was looking for a new pastor. The region he spoke of was a beautiful dairy-rich area of New Zealand. I knew of one church in this region that was engaged in a pastoral search but I was aware that this church had a chequered history in dealings with pastors and that the last one had been dismissed under a cloud. The thought of another bad church experience was more than I was able to contemplate.

One evening, as Karen and I once again talked of our hopes and fears, I said, 'I've always loved Cambridge,' which was a beautiful small town in the region in question. 'If the church there was up for grabs I'd be keen, but I'm sure it isn't.'

Remarkably, within 24 hours the pastor from the Cambridge church had called and invited us to come and have a look at the fellowship he was about to depart from. So we travelled to Cambridge to both view and be viewed. The end result was that we were asked to be the pastors of that small group of about 35 to 45 people.

In June of 1980, still battle weary and gun-shy from our first ministry experience, we made the five-hour journey to our new home and church. In those first months (probably *years*, if the truth be known) our little congregation ministered more to us than we did to them. They loved us towards healing and towards believing again that the church could be a safe community. I think we needed to experience that truth personally before we could proclaim it with any conviction.

The first few months away from Dave were a mixture of trying to forget and trying to understand – two desires that seemed to work against each other.

I vividly recall receiving a moment of clarity from God after I asked, probably for the umpteenth time, 'What was that all about Lord? Why did we have to go through those seven years?'

It seemed to me that the Lord posed me a question, 'Why did I send Jacob to Laban?'

I immediately remembered the conversation between my friend Mark and the youth conference speaker, and the reported answer I had placed in the later-to-be-considered-file. He too had referenced the story of Jacob and Laban (Genesis 29). Perhaps this was the time for it to be considered.

I knew the answer to God's question in a fraction of a second, though I took some time to unpack it fully.

Jacob was a crook; a lovable crook; a crook with a heart for God and spiritual things; but a crook nonetheless. He took, by stealth, his brother's birthright and then deceived his aged father into giving him his brother's blessing. Jacob needed an encounter that would show him his own twisted ugliness. God arranged it in the form of Laban. Laban proved to be, as R. Paul Stevens calls it, a 'God-polished mirror' to Jacob.[1] In the face of Uncle Laban, Jacob, for 20 long years, encountered a close approximation of himself.

If Jacob was a crook, Laban was a crook *par excellence*.

Laban played Jacob at his own game and, at least in the first half of the story, won hands down. He made Jacob serve seven years for Rachel's hand in marriage, and then gave him Leah instead. Then he extracted another seven years out of Jacob for Rachel. He changed Jacob's wages ten times (Genesis 31:7). At every turn, these two tricksters matched wits with each other and attempted to gain the upper hand in a two-decade-long struggle.

After 20 years of being given the run-around, Jacob had had his fill. As he travelled back to his homeland, he wrestled with a man at the Brook Jabbok (Genesis 32). Actually, the text states that 'a man wrestled with Jacob,' rather than the other way around. If I wrestle with a man, then I seek something from him; if a man wrestles with me, then he is seeking something from me. God was seeking something from Jacob.

The word *Jabbok* in the Hebrew means 'pouring' or 'emptying out,' which is very appropriate. I think God was seeking to bring Jacob to a place of recognition and realisation; of emptying Jacob out of this deep propensity to resort to trickery in obtaining what he wanted.

As dawn approached, the mysterious wrestler asked Jacob, 'What is your name?' This was more than just some belated introduction – 'We've been wrestling all night and we haven't even been introduced!'

Rather, it was a profound question that probed Jacob's identity: 'Who are you at the deepest level?'

In the Old Testament, a name was often prophetic of, or a testament to, a person's character or nature. Jacob's name meant 'supplanter, deceiver.'

When Jacob answered the wrestler's question, I imagine him spitting it out with venom, 'I am *Jacob* and I hate it!' He had come to the end of himself and now desperately sought transformation.

When God asked me, 'Why did I send Jacob to Laban?'

I immediately understood the reason: to place Jacob in front of a mirror so that he could know himself. Then I felt God ask another, much deeper and, to me, somewhat more sinister question,

'Why did I send you to an insecure man?'

I scrambled around for a pass-card in the hopes of avoiding the question and its painful implication – anything to throw the spotlight off the issue I knew was about to be highlighted. But I thought better of it.

'Because I too am an insecure man,' I answered, somewhat reluctantly and definitely without much conviction.

'You had to understand what insecurity is and how destructive it is, or you could end up doing to others as Dave has done to you.'

I protested with a vehemence but I instantly regretted the words that escaped my lips, 'I would never do that; I am not like him!'

'No,' the Lord said firmly, 'you're much more sophisticated aren't you?'

Busted! I knew deep in my heart that I was a Jacob, and just before you're tempted to feel sorry for me, let me say that you are a Jacob too. We all are.

Jeremiah 17:9 is an oft-quoted passage, 'The heart is deceitful above all things, and desperately wicked: who can know it?' (KJV). The Hebrew word translated here as 'deceitful' is *aqob*. It is the basis for the name Jacob.

Jeremiah 17:9 could literally read, 'The heart is *Jacobful* or *Jacob-like...*' That's true of all our hearts.

During the next few weeks after this moment of clarity, God revealed to me the meaning of the season we had passed through.

I was, at that time, taking the opportunity to read my way through a list of books that Dave had instructed us not to read. I guess this was my slightly infantile way of striking a blow for freedom – asserting my independence like a toddler pushing their parent away.

One of these 'banned books' was a little gem, *A Tale of Three Kings* by Gene Edwards. This portion hit me like a sledgehammer:

> I'm in David's situation, and I am in agony. What do I do when the kingdom I am in is ruled by a spear-wielding king? What does a man do in the midst of a knife throwing contest?
>
> Well if you didn't like the question found in the last chapter, you won't like the answer found in this one.
>
> The answer is, 'You get stabbed to death.'
>
> 'What is the necessity of that? Or the good of it?'

You have your eyes on the wrong King Saul. As long as you look at your king, you will blame him and him alone for your present hell. Be careful, for God has His eyes fastened sharply on another King Saul. Not the visible one standing up there throwing spears. No, God is looking at another King Saul. One just as bad – or worse. God is looking at the King Saul in you.

'In me?'

Saul is in your bloodstream, in the marrow of your bones, He makes up the very flesh and muscle of your heart. He is mixed into your soul. He inhabits the nuclei of your atoms.

King Saul is one with you.

You are King Saul.

He breathes in the lungs and beats in the breast of us all. There is only one way to get rid of him. He must be annihilated.

You may not particularly find this to be a compliment, but at least you know why God put you under someone who might just be King Saul.

David the sheepherder would have grown up to be King Saul II, except that God cut away the Saul in David's heart. The operation, by the way, took years and was a brutalising experience that almost killed the patient. And what were the scalpel and tongs God used to remove this inner Saul?

God used the outer Saul.

King Saul sought to destroy David, but his only success was that he became the handmaiden of God to put to

> death the Saul who roamed about in the caverns of David's own heart.
>
> Yes, it is true that David was virtually destroyed in the process, but this had to be. Otherwise the Saul in him would have survived.
>
> David accepted his fate. He embraced the cruel circumstances. He lifted no hand nor offered resistance. Nor did he grandstand his piety. Silently, privately, he bore the crucibles. Because of this he was deeply wounded. His whole inner being was mutilated. His personality was altered. When the gore was over, David was barely recognisable.'[2]

As I sat contemplating what I had read, the Lord reinforced His earlier statement to me, 'This was a needful school of the Spirit for you.'

In the intervening years since that school, I have had the wonderful and terrible privilege of ministering to leaders in numerous countries. One of the topics I always teach on is insecurity.

I never cease to be amazed at how people respond when the message strikes home.

In America I've been asked, 'Did you have a word of knowledge about me and my situation?' In the Philippines I was asked, 'Are you a prophet?' Missionaries from Central Asia asked if I had managed to hack into the personnel files on the computer system of the organisation they worked for.

Once, in the north-east of India, high up in the Himalayan foothills, I talked on the subject of insecurity and found myself embroiled in unforeseen controversy.

As I finished my message, an obviously irate, aged pastor rose to his feet.

'I want to say something that I do not want to have translated. I don't want our speaker in on this discussion.'

You know something is desperately wrong when a normally hospitable people speak like that. For the next ten minutes, the pastor talked heatedly in his local dialect as I sat uncomfortably, wondering, as I invariably do at some point in almost every trip, 'Why do I do this?'

Finally, a woman rose to her feet and, in English, upbraided those present for their rudeness. 'We do our speaker a great disservice,' she started. 'I am going to tell him what you have been saying.' She then proceeded to recap the discussion for my benefit.

'The first speaker challenged your right as a stranger to come to our region and speak so pointedly about our local problem.'

He believed that I had somehow gained inside information about the particular difficulties pastors and people in this remote region had with insecurity, and that I had used it to embarrass him.

I was able to apologise for any difficulty I had caused but also point out that what he thought was a regional problem was, in fact, a human one.

So many of us have misused our leadership positions in an attempt to somehow *find* emotional wholeness, rather than using those positions as a platform to *express it*. This misuse often occurs almost subconsciously.

Let me say, quite frankly, and perhaps a touch brutally, that some of us are simply too insecure – too emotionally hungry – to be safe in leadership.

I suspect the tendency for most of us when we hear a message like this is to immediately do an internal audit, 'Do I have insecurity or don't I?'

Can I suggest that a better way of approaching the issue is to see insecurity as a spectrum? Rather than asking, 'Do I have it or not?' it is better to ask, 'How much do I have and how debilitating is it?'

We all battle with some level of insecurity. The question is, where on the spectrum do I find myself?

When Adam and Eve walked with God in the garden before the fall, they were secure. They knew where they stood in God's affection and purposes and, unclouded by sin, they knew where they stood with each other. Sin changed that dramatically.

> And they heard the voice of the Lord God walking in the garden in the cool of the day: and Adam and his wife hid themselves from the presence of the Lord God amongst the trees of the garden. And the Lord God called unto Adam, and said unto him, Where art thou?
>
> And he said, I heard thy voice in the garden, and I was afraid, because I was naked; and I hid myself (Genesis 3:8-10 KJV).

Adam is now in hiding, acutely aware of his nakedness and

vulnerability, unsure of where he stands with God and how God feels about him. He is now deeply insecure.

This Adamic propensity to insecurity is, for most of us, heightened by life's experiences. Even in the best of families – let alone the more dysfunctional ones – we are wounded by words, attitudes and events that deepen the wound and leave us struggling to secure and prove our worth.

For many of us, as we grew up, our identity became wedded to our achievements. If we achieved, then we imagined that we were somehow worthwhile and valuable; if we failed, we felt worthless and insignificant.

This tendency is exacerbated by the fact that we instinctively compare our achievements with those of the people around us. It's not our achievements in and of themselves, but how these achievements rate alongside those of our siblings and peers that determine our value.

Insecurity fuels a spirit of competition and is essentially competitive by nature. So if someone achieves more significantly than we do, we assume that they are more valuable and significant than we are. This can turn to envy and jealousy.

As destructive and, quite frankly, as demonic (James 3:14-15) as envy and jealousy can be, I suspect they are actually a symptom of a deeper problem. They function as a barometer that reveals the level of our insecurity.

Author Dan Allender comments,

> Envy arises because we are not grateful for how God has written our world or for how he has blessed us. Envy comes from a sense of inadequacy and emptiness rooted

> in our woundedness. The more a person is driven by emptiness and inadequacy, the more self centred and violent that person will become.[3]

Insecurity ensures that we are unable to follow through on Paul's injunction to rejoice with those who rejoice and weep with those who weep (Romans 12:15). In fact we will often function in exactly the opposite manner.

When someone else, especially if they work in a similar field, is weeping, the insecure find themselves rejoicing (inwardly if not outwardly). Or, if the other is rejoicing and experiencing a degree of success and prominence, the insecure will experience annoyance and bitter feelings. The story of King Saul is a dramatic illustration of the destructive effects of insecurity run amok, in his own life and in the lives of those he was called to lead. As long as Saul is the biggest dog in the kennel, all is well. Provided no one is out performing him – and his superior performance and actions lead him to believe that he is the most important and most significant leader in the kingdom – all is peaceful and harmonious.

But what happens when God brings David to an insecure Saul? Saul is happy enough to have David around, brightening up the demeanour of the office with his sweet songs and skilful musicianship, but as soon as David slays Goliath and the maidens start singing, then you have a recipe for trouble. Saul's 'envy barometer' goes off the scale. His insecurity immediately registers that David is a threat – a threat that has to be removed. 'And so he was jealous and suspicious of David from that day on' (1 Samuel 18:9, GNT).

My deep conviction is that leaders are raised up by God in order to serve His people and foster a culture that inevitably leads to the release of the dreams that the Holy Spirit has put in the people's hearts. We are called to serve the Davids that God has placed in our care; to do our best to release them to be all they can be, rather than spending our energy and emotional resources defending our title and turf from the perceived threat we think they represent.

Insecure leaders tend to act like *owners,* rather than understanding that they are merely *stewards*.

Saul functioned like an owner and sought to protect what he mistakenly perceived to be his. David, by contrast, understood himself to be a steward, even when his kingdom was threatened by Absalom. He gave the young pretender a level of latitude that his predecessor would never have allowed. David was secure in the knowledge that it wasn't *his* kingdom to defend in the first place.

Leadership isn't the end; it's the means to the end. In many cases, leaders have turned the tables and people are valued only in as much as they serve the leader's dream.

2 Samuel 5:12 provides us with a reality check: 'And David perceived that the LORD had established him king over Israel, and that he had exalted his kingdom *for his people Israel's sake*' (KJV, emphasis added).

David realised that all of God's dealings in his heart – the enlargement and success God gave him – had a bigger purpose beyond personal exaltation; it was all for the sake of the people of God.

Paul the Apostle was possessed of a similar conviction. In writing to the church at Colossae he states, 'Whereof I am made a minister, according to the dispensation of God *which is given to me for you,* to fulfil the word of God…' (Colossians 1:25 KJV, emphasis added)

J B Philips translates the italicised portion, 'a commission granted to me for your benefit.' The Amplified Bible has, 'entrusted to me for you as its object and for your benefit.'

Both David and Paul understood they were servants of God and that all God had done in and through their lives was ultimately for the sake of serving His people.

It is extremely difficult for an insecure person to serve in a sustained manner since they are often preoccupied with climbing the ladder of success.

Unfortunately, insecurity is often coupled with an illicit concern for personal notoriety. Saul was more concerned about image management than he was about the fact that he had disobeyed God. 'Saul said, "I did sin, but please honour me in front of the leaders of the army and the people of Israel. Come back with me, so I can worship the LORD your God."' (1 Samuel 15:30 CEV)

It's impossible to stoop in servanthood and stretch towards notoriety at the same time. Jesus' disciples constantly fought about who was the greatest among them, and were therefore unwilling and unable to take the position of the servant who washed the others' feet on the eve of the Passover.

As they entered the room that fateful evening, each of them would have been acutely aware of the task that had been left undone. Foot-washing was customarily the responsibility of the household's lowest servant. The task involved washing the daily accumulation of dust and dirt off the feet of the invited guests.

In their quest for position and prominence within the group, the disciples had often disputed the pecking order of perceived greatness. Jesus had sought to address their mistaken perceptions on numerous occasions but it seems the lesson hadn't taken. Because their concept of greatness was inextricably linked with achievement and outward position, none of them were willing to undertake the foot-washer role. In their befuddled understanding, to *do menial* was to *be menial.*

Peter, James and John were the obvious frontrunners in the race to be Jesus' favourite. Perhaps some of the others, realising they didn't have a shot at the top spot, had simply determined not to be the last of the 'also rans'.

Richard Foster astutely comments,

> Whenever there is trouble over the greatest there is trouble over the least. This is the crux of the matter for most of us isn't it? Most of us know we'll never be the greatest, just don't let us be the least.[4]

When supper was over, Jesus rose and took the towel and taught them a lesson that I suspect finally broke the spell that the lifelong quest for human greatness had cast over them.

> Now before the feast of the passover, when Jesus *knew* that his hour was come that he should depart out of this world unto the Father, having loved his own which were in the world, he loved them unto the end. And supper being ended, the devil having now put into the heart of Judas Iscariot, Simon's son, to betray him; Jesus *knowing* that the Father had given all things into his hands, and that he was come from God, and went to God; He riseth from supper, and laid aside his garments; and took a towel, and girded himself. After that he poureth water into a bason, and began to wash the disciples' feet, and to wipe them with the towel wherewith he was girded (John 13:1-5 KJV, emphasis added).

I think the key words of this passage are *know* (v1) and *knowing* (v3). Jesus knew something the disciples didn't, and this knowledge released him to serve when they could not.

Jesus was secure in His Father's love and was certain of the Father's faithfulness and purpose. He had heard His Father's voice affirming Him on several occasions, including at His baptism (Matthew 3:17) and at the Mount of Transfiguration (Matthew 17:5). These experiences furnished a clear, core identity for the human Jesus.

His security was based on what His Father had said and therefore He did not have to be secured by any accomplishments or by any particular position. Secure in being the Son of God, He did not need to strive for position in order to prove to others who He was. This released Him to serve; to do the lowly and the menial. His self-esteem was not under threat.

E Stanley Jones once commented,

> Conscious of being great with an ultimate greatness he could afford to be humble. Real humility is not rooted in a sense of humiliation; it's rooted in a sense of being inwardly great. The little person [read 'insecure'] dare not be humble; it would give away his littleness. He has to act a part, a part of being great in order to compensate for being small. The one who is truly great doesn't have to act a part; he has nothing to keep up. He is great and therefore is released to do the lowly.[5]

One of the best illustrations of this principle is contained in Langdon Gilkey's exceptional book, *The Shantung Compound.*

Gilkey's true story is set in China during World War II. The European population had been rounded up by the Japanese and herded into camps to be detained for the duration of the war. Gilkey describes the unpleasant task of cleaning the latrines in the overcrowded camp.

> The only women in camp who deliberately avoided this latrine duty were two Russian women married, respectively to a wealthy American and a wealthy Briton. The point certainly was not that they were Russian. They hired other Russian women to do these chores for them... and it was a wonderful Russian woman married to a British professor ...who voluntarily took on the odorous and bruising task of running this cleanup crew for the women's latrines. Obviously the cause of their

> refusal was that they were both hoping to move up socially into colonial society and out of the nothingness of refugee society. They had, one could not but guess, married these well-to-do men for their wealth and their prestige. They did not intend to lose all this newly gained social status by falling back into the very kind of life they had left behind them. For them, if there was any one symbol of that old life, it was the job of taking care of the women's conveniences. The irony of this was intensified by the fact that the socially prominent wives of the high-ranking British business officials would never have dreamed of refusing to do this work, once it became a recognised form of community service. While the two women who aspired to grandeur were too proud and too insecure to do it, the British possessors of status were too proud and too secure to refuse.[6]

Insecure leaders are like the two Russian women. Trying so desperately to prove to all and sundry that they are worthy of being followed, they refuse to do the one thing that would inspire potential followers – serve.

I believe that as followers of Christ, we must have core identity experiences that secure us in God's love and faithfulness. The good news is that God is abundantly able and willing to give these experiences.

We need to hear the Father's voice, whether it be through our study of the Scriptures (perhaps the most common method used by the Holy Spirit), or in one of the many other ways He has at His disposal, affirming that we are His beloved children.

Secured by these encounters, we are free to minister out of acceptance rather than being driven to seek acceptance through ministry.

We need to experience what Paul spoke of in Ephesians 3:16-19.

> That he would grant you, according to the riches of his glory, to be strengthened with might by his Spirit in the inner man; That Christ may dwell in your hearts by faith; that ye, being *rooted and grounded in love,* May be able to comprehend with all saints what is the breadth, and length, and depth, and height; And to know the love of Christ, which passeth knowledge, that ye might be filled with all the fulness of God (KJV, emphasis added).

The nineteenth century idealist philosopher G W F Hegel once famously commented, 'The owl of Minerva flies only as dusk falls.'[7] What Hegel meant was that we only gain wisdom and understanding in retrospect, when a particular period comes to an end. Things look different with the benefit of hindsight. The Danish philosopher, Søren Kierkegaard said something similar when he commented that we live life going forward but understand it looking backwards.

This was certainly true for Karen and me in the difficult season we had just passed through.

Dealing with the 'Jacob' of insecurity in my own heart was, and continues to be, an ongoing process. There are periods when I function as if insecurity is a conquered issue of my past. But before long, I will be faced with some incident that shows me quite clearly my weakness remains. If allowed, my insecurity will influence and taint the decisions I make and the direction I take. As all leaders must, I seek, by God's grace, to move along the spectrum towards wholeness and healing.

CHAPTER 4

The 'Vision Thing'

Karen and I spent the next 11 and a half years pastoring the fellowship in Cambridge. We worked out our ideas of what church was, and wasn't, on that unsuspecting and mostly innocent group of saints. I am often amazed, and always thankful, as I look back at the sermons I preached and the ideas I hatched during that period; we owe the continuation of our ministry there to the people's kindness, pity and tolerance.

I realise that, in many respects, the philosophy I initially developed concerning church life and ministry was reactionary. I was determined not to be like Dave and sought to 'do church' in a very different way. Reaction always spawns its own set of problems and the time we had in Cambridge was, in hindsight, really about allowing our reactionary swings to slow down and begin to centre, so I could find a better middle ground. It took me that decade and a bit to formulate a philosophy of ministry which I felt was scriptural, workable and healthy.

One of the early issues I grappled with – a grappling that lasted many years – was the whole issue of developing a leadership vision for the church; of needing to become the kind of inspiring, visionary leader that people would want to follow. I know I'm not alone in this struggle.

I can't begin to list the number of conferences I have attended and the messages I have heard about the need for leaders to have a vision and to effectively communicate that vision to the people they lead.

The classic scripture from Proverbs 29:18, 'Where there is no vision, the people perish…' had appeared in so many sermons that it had become an unchallenged truism in my thinking.

I remember one speaker urging us to go, 'Moses-like', up the mountain and obtain from heaven 'the pattern' for our local church setting. If we would then build 'according to this pattern,' we would be assured of divine success.

Buoyed by such messages, I had strapped on my sandals and, in as Moses-like fashion as I could muster, had gone up the mountain. Actually, our local 'mountain' was only a moderately-sized hill, and I drove to the top, which I felt somewhat guilty about and wondered if driving might somehow disqualify me from the possibility of divine insight altogether. These days, I often joke that I went up the mountain to get the divine pattern but all I came back with was frostbite.

It took many years, and not a little angst, to finally come to the conclusion that I was seeking something that wasn't the axiom I had assumed it to be. I have come to the conclusion that, at least in the circles in which I moved, the vision thing had been completely overcooked.

Perhaps the speakers I listened to so attentively didn't mean what I assumed they meant when they talked about vision. But it appeared that I wasn't the only one that came away from these conferences with the idea that it was my particular responsibility, as a leader, to get from God some kind of special blueprint for the church I was leading. As I understood it, this blueprint would tell me what should be happening in ministry, outreach, social programming, building plans, church size and so forth.

I came away with the concept that in order to be a 'visionary leader' I really needed to aspire to be a highly gifted individual, oozing charisma, spiritually dynamic, with a larger-than-life personality (a white suit and shoes could possibly be an advantage as well) and with an ability to communicate my dream in a way that would galvanise the masses towards God's preferred future. Dynamic leaders like that would 'en-vision' as many helpers as they could, in order to make the dream come true.

Jim Collins, in his superb leadership book, *Good to Great*, calls these leaders, 'The genius with a thousand helpers.'[1]

One problem loomed large for me in this scenario: I was painfully aware that I was no genius. I wasn't by nature a larger-than-life personality and, to make matters worse, I hated white suits and white shoes!

Dave had told me several times over the years that I would never be a 'number one leader', since I just didn't have an 'outgoing personality with the required initiative and charisma'.

For the first few years of ministry in Cambridge, I agonised over the awareness that I wasn't in possession of a divine, mountain-top vision for the church I led. I assumed that I was somehow inadequate as a leader. I prayed longer and fasted more often, but still no pattern from heaven – just sore knees and an empty stomach.

At this point in their journey, leaders who struggle as I did face a huge challenge; do we force the issue and manufacture a vision or do we honestly re-examine our perspective on the whole vision-based model of ministry?

A friend of mine had to give a devotional talk on one occasion. He began by saying, 'I asked God for a word this morning. He didn't give me one, so I made this one up.' Very candid! Truth be told, I suspect many of us are in the same boat when it comes to vision, minus my friend's level of honesty.

Feeling uncomfortable with the idea of coming up with a vision of my own devising, I instead determined to reassess the message I had believed and the role of vision in the task of spiritual leadership. While teaching a series of messages on Joseph, some light began to dawn for me. Joseph is one of my favourite Bible characters. I love that young dreamer; his purity, his integrity, his ability to persevere, his forgiveness – truly inspiring. As I approached the end of the teaching series and was talking about Joseph's reunion with his brothers, it struck me that all that God had done in this young man's life was for the purpose of preserving the lives, and thereby the dreams, of his brethren (Genesis 45:5, 50:20).

The ultimate purpose of *his* dreams was to release *theirs*.

As I began to contemplate this idea in relation to New Testament leadership, it occurred to me that it wasn't my responsibility to have all the dreams, but rather to minister and lead in such a way that the dreams God had put in the hearts of others would come to fruition.

I didn't have to have all the visions and dreams for the community; I had to minister in order to create a community of dreamers.

I didn't have to possess any particular kind of personality – larger-than-life or otherwise. I didn't have to ooze charisma or have divine insight into the future of the church. But I did need to have an absolute commitment to serving the dreams that God had put in the hearts of the people I led.

As I contemplated this alternative model of ministry, Ephesians 4 came alive to me.

> And he gave some, apostles; and some, prophets; and some, evangelists; and some, pastors and teachers; *For the perfecting of the saints*, for the work of the ministry, for the edifying of the body of Christ: Till we all come in the unity of the faith, and of the knowledge of the Son of God, unto a perfect man, unto the measure of the stature of the fullness of Christ: That we henceforth be no more children, tossed to and fro, and carried about with every wind of doctrine, by the sleight of men, and cunning craftiness, whereby they lie in wait to deceive; But speaking the truth in love, may grow up into him in all things, which is the head, even Christ: From whom the whole body fitly joined together and compacted by that which every joint supplieth, according to the effectual working in the measure of every part, maketh increase of the body unto the edifying of itself in love (Ephesians 4:11-16 KJV, emphasis added).

It was clear to me that the role of leadership was not to do the work of the ministry, but to develop (perfect – *katartismos* in Greek) and release the people so that they could minister in whatever field God had positioned and gifted them.

These days, when people ask the question (it's nearly always churched people looking for another church, since the unchurched would never think of asking it), 'What is your vision?'

I respond, 'My vision is to fulfil yours; so what's *your* vision?'

This response is almost always followed by a confused silence. In truth, people are asking about my vision to determine whether I am a genius worthy of their support. Is my vision sufficiently great and inspiring that they will endorse it with their attendance and financial giving?

The thought that God might have placed dreams in their own hearts either hasn't occurred to them at all, or has been buried by a model of church life that has reduced them to passive spectators looking for a genius to follow.

The things we have too often left for the genius to concoct while alone on the mountaintop – namely ministry ideas, outreach programmes, social-justice initiatives and so on – are instead best developed by ordinary people who have a dream and a passion for them. We need secure leaders who can encourage and enable people to follow through on ideas that are far beyond anything the leader could dream up by him or herself.

Len Sweet, in his book *Nudge,* comments,

> A 'vision' is too often 'done' to an institution by a leader, making it a passive rather than a participatory process. In some ways we need to learn how not to have a vision; even to make things purposively vague, which allows

everyone space to shape the vision so they are not treated as objects but as subjects.[2]

Because vision thinking is so ingrained in our perspective of leadership, the next question is inevitable: 'If my role as a leader is not to come up with the dream and the vision, what am I supposed to do; what is my role?'

As leaders, I think we are first and foremost 'environmental architects.' We are responsible to create and develop healthy environments in which dreams can be safely pursued.

At this point I can almost hear frustrated leaders asking, 'Are you suggesting that there is no place for vision and for visionary leaders? That is preposterous!'

Obviously I am not trying to overthrow or in any way invalidate the wisdom of a vast multitude of thoughtful writers and students of leadership theory. Without doubt, vision has its place and visionary leaders have, and will continue to have, a huge role in organisations of all kinds, including churches.

I am suggesting, however, that vision isn't the only thing, or even perhaps necessarily the most important ingredient in a leader's arsenal. While vision is vital for an organisation or church to go forward, I don't think it is the sole responsibility of the leader to have it all or labour under the impossible burden of being its only source.

Jim Collins in his book, *Good to Great*, identified the kinds of leaders that are responsible for the development of enduring, top performing companies. He made a differentiation between two types of leaders. One he called Level 4 leaders, and the second group, Level 5 leaders. Level 4 leaders were typically charismatic, vision-driven personalities. While these people were often able to build vibrant companies, the research showed that they were rarely able to produce enduring companies that lasted beyond their tenure. Somewhat counter-intuitively, the research revealed that such leaders were often negatively correlated with the building of truly visionary companies.

It seems that the kind of leadership that is often promoted as a basic necessity for a great church may in fact be a liability in the long run.

Level 5 leaders, those who Collins and his team identified as developers of enduring, top-performing companies, were not especially characterised by either charisma or vision. They were people whose chief characteristics were their desire and determination to create environments in which creative employees could safely dream and innovate. So often our thinking gravitates to either/or categories. In this case, either the leader has the vision or we develop a culture in which the people develop visionary ideas. Which is it? Perhaps the answer is both! Perhaps we can embrace the 'genius of the and', rather than be forced to chose between alternatives.

There is a great need to find a place of balance between imposing vision from above and allowing vision to bubble up from beneath. In his book *Intuitive Leadership,* Tim Keel speaks about Emergence Theory.

Emergence theory is a developing branch of science

> that states that coherent patterns exist and arise from interactions among simple objects when there is a *commingling of bottom up and top down processes*. In simple terms, this theory states that life emerges in unique ways when an environment is created that allows for bottom up and top down interactions (emphasis added).[3]

If we can imagine top down visionary leadership interacting and commingling with the bottom up visions and dreams of the congregation, then perhaps spiritual life can emerge in unique and powerful ways that are not possible when we limit the flow of vision to one direction only.

Keel goes on to say,

> Rather than operating with a predetermined direction set from the top down (*my definition of vision*) emergent structures develop as the result of collective behaviours and interactions among many diverse players… these interactive and iterative processes can help cultivate cultures that allow for experimentation and engagement (emphasis added).[4]

As I look back on Gateway's journey over the last 20 years (more about how we got there a bit later in this book), I am very aware that some of the most fruitful and life-producing ventures that we have engaged in have come from the dreams and visions, not of positional leaders, but of passionate saints who have felt the freedom and permission to step forward and follow through on something that they felt God had put in their hearts.

My great challenge as a leader has been to be secure enough to allow them to experiment and succeed, and to purposefully develop a culture in which more and more people would feel the freedom and permission to follow their dreams.

CHAPTER 5

The Leader as an 'Environmental Architect'

Being released from the intolerable (at least for me) burden of being the 'charismatic visionary,' was unspeakably liberating. In some respects, however, it was replaced with an even more challenging task – one of building a healthy culture that would encourage the emergence of the ministry dreams of the people we led. What would such a culture look like? What were the tools I had at my disposal to build such a culture?

Corporate culture is to an organisation what personality is to an individual. We all have one. Some are pleasant and alluring; others obnoxious and off-putting. As I've suggested, I think the leader's prime responsibility is to ensure the culture we develop in our churches is of the alluring variety.

Culture consists of tangibles and intangibles – of outward behaviour and deeply held, often unarticulated, values. It surrounds us – and all we do, see and understand is mediated to us through our cultural environment and the world-view it provides.

Culture is largely unnoticed and therefore often unexamined. Its invisibility actually makes it more powerful. Samuel Chand, in his book *Cracking Your Church's Culture,* amusingly comments, 'Toxic culture is like carbon monoxide; you don't see it or smell it, but you wake up dead.'[1]

Without an awareness and understanding of culture, many of our attempts at transforming our churches will be limited to tangible externals – the *how* things are done, rather than the *why*. We end up with the frustration of having everything changed and nothing different.

Over the last decade or so, I have noticed a significant emphasis on 'excellence' in church circles. Obviously I'm not against such a call per se. I'm not some pastoral Bart Simpson whose brief is to strive for mediocrity. But I am convinced that unless we attend to the deeper, undergirding elements of church culture, the drive to excellence may not have the effects we desire.

Imagine a restaurant that has a vision for culinary excellence. They advertise this fact and direct all their efforts towards providing discerning patrons with the finest cuisine. If all goes to plan, the food will be long remembered and satisfied customers will return time and again, hopefully with their friends in tow.

The aim for culinary excellence is laudable, but as any restaurateur worth his or her salt knows, the dish put before the patron is only one part (albeit a vital part) of a bigger picture. The ambience of the venue, the warmth of the staff, and the cleanliness of the surroundings will mean as much, maybe more, than the dish itself. For a patron, the abruptness, distraction or even the plain rudeness of the staff, the stains on the tablecloth or the cutlery, and the dirt under the fingernails of the waiter or waitress will trump the excellence of the food.

The cuisine may be excellent, but it's the other things that amount to *culture*.

Chand suggests that 'Culture, not vision or strategy, is the most powerful factor in any organization.'[2]

Many churches have visions and strategies that will never gain traction simply because their culture is such that it will trump their strategy.

Dick Clark, Executive Chairman of Merk Pharmaceuticals once quipped, 'Culture eats strategy for lunch.'

Young leaders often step into an already functioning organisation and seek to lead without any sense of its existing ethos. They quickly find themselves running into a brick wall and wonder why their leadership efforts and great ideas are ineffective. When a culture and a leader clash, unless the leader is very aware of what they are up against and is intentional in how they address the issues, culture wins every time.

Edgar H Schein has written profoundly about the culture of organisations. I think his book, *Organizational Culture and Leadership*, is a must read for any budding leader.

Schein states, 'Leaders as entrepreneurs are the main architects of culture and ... after cultures are formed they influence the kind of leadership that is possible.'[3]

In other words, leaders build culture and then culture builds leadership. Once the culture is established, it determines the criteria for who can or cannot become a leader within the organisation.

If Schein is correct in his assessment of the importance of culture in an organisation, then it is imperative that leaders identify and build culture very intentionally and very wisely.

How can we go about developing, or possibly bringing change to, the culture of our leadership situation? What are the tools we have at our disposal?

It is my conviction that the fundamental building block of a healthy culture will be the value system that you as a leader teach and embody. Much of the rest of this book will unpack that idea.

Lyle Schaller, a well known church consultant, has noted, 'The most important single element of a corporate congregational or denominational culture is its value system.'[4]

In his book *Leadership is an Art*, Max De Pree agrees with Schaller and states,

> Leaders need to be concerned with the institutional value system which after all leads to the purposes and standards that guide the practices of the people in the institution... those values should shape our corporate and individual behaviour.[5]

Our values are the deep, foundational moral and ethical convictions that will guide and determine our behaviour, and serve to fashion the ethos of the churches we lead as we pursue our vision.

Your values are your personal non-negotiables. They are the things in your life that are 'not for sale.'

I recall hearing a story of a businessman on a flight. He

was seated besides a stunningly attractive young woman. After some small talk around destinations and occupations, the business man brazenly asked the young lady if she would sleep with him if he paid her a million dollars. Initially outraged by his impertinent suggestion she sat in sullen silence. The temptation of a million dollars in her bank account progressively overwhelmed any scruples she may have had about sleeping with a strange man so she broke the silence and said, 'Alright I'll do it.'

He looked at her and said, 'Will you do it for $100?'

She exploded in anger, 'What do you think I am?'

He calmly replied, 'Madam, we have already established what you are. We are simply haggling over the price.'

For far too many people there is nothing that is not for sale.

Oz Guinness observes,

> Not everything can or should be given a market price. The sign of a good society is the level and number of things that are acknowledged to be beyond market values and thus appreciated for their own sake and not for extrinsic, especially financial rewards. The line between 'for sale,' and 'not for sale,' is a key indication of a nation's values.[6]

Our culture rests on, and is developed out of, deep foundational values.

I believe every leader should have an intentionally developed and clearly articulated set of values that guide his or her life and ministry. We shape our journey and view our goals through the matrix of these values. They are things that are not for sale and will not be surrendered – even if this means we'll ultimately fall short of some objective. Values are more important than achievements.

Our common scriptural foundations will, I think, provide a basic consistency of values among believers, but the way we express, prioritise and articulate them will differ from individual to individual and from church to church. I am not mandating that the particular values that I emphasise and will unpack through the remainder of the book need be exactly the same for you. You must find your own set of values and let them be part of your unique identity.

Once the value set is in place and is clear then we are in a position to go about being intentional in developing the culture of our church.

As environmental architects, there are tools at our disposal by which we are able to create or recreate culture.

The first indispensable tool is our own life well-lived. As a leader, the manner in which you live will be perhaps the most significant factor in creating the ethos of the environment where you serve.

Schein comments, 'Culture is ultimately created, embedded, evolved and ultimately manipulated by leaders.'[7] I would want to revise that to, 'by the character or life of the leader.'

He goes on to say that a leader's 'visible behaviour has great value for communicating assumptions and values to other members, especially newcomers.'

Leaders wield influence. It has been noted by many astute observers that organisations tend to become the lengthened shadow of their leaders; the culture of the organisation becomes an exaggerated form of the leader's own character.

Paul advised Timothy to set an example in the way he lived. 'Let no one despise your youth, but *be an example* to the believers, in word, in conduct, in love, in spirit, in faith, in purity' (1 Timothy 4:12 MKJV, emphasis added).

The Greek word translated as 'example' is *tupos*. It conveys the idea of a stamp, print or pattern formed by the pressure of one object on another. Our character impresses itself on those we lead, for good or ill.

Robert Murray McCheyne, the great Scottish preacher, once commented, 'My people's greatest need is my personal holiness.'

He understood that, in fashioning the culture around us, what we teach comes a distant second to who we are as people. We can teach what we *know*, but ultimately we always reproduce what we *are*. The natural law of reproduction is that like produces like.

We will be unable, for example, to build and sustain a culture of generosity if we are stingy. We won't see a culture of warmth and welcome develop if we are aloof and withdrawn. If we're not personally devoted, then there's no point berating our people for their lack of authentic spirituality.

General Booth, founder of the Salvation Army, once told his officers in strong terms that if they wanted their people to bleed then they would need to *haemorrhage*.

E M Bounds observed that, 'Our preaching is life giving if we are life giving; the sermon is forceful only if we are forceful. It is holy if we are holy and it is full of unction only if we are full of unction.'[8]

Leadership cannot rise in its effectiveness above the character and values of the man or woman seeking to lead. We must live out our values if they are ever to be reproduced.

A second powerful tool in our arsenal is the pulpit. We lead and create culture through our public communication. The pulpit is a place of significant influence. Karen often tells me that rather than simply teaching from the pulpit, I lead from that position.

I wasn't fully aware of this in the early days of my ministry. I simply assumed that the pulpit was the place from which the Word of God was to be taught – hopefully clearly and well. I think I imagined that preaching would be somehow separate from me, rather than an extension of me.

God doesn't reject our flesh, but instead clothes Himself in it. As you read the four Gospels you become aware that the personality of each writer isn't divinely suspended and excluded from the communication process. The Holy Spirit uses Luke's knowledge of medicine and love of history, and weaves those things into the sacred text. He harnesses John's tender spirituality to probe the depths of the character of the divine Logos. He allows Mark's realism and no nonsense pragmatism to shine through.

As you read Matthew's Gospel, it isn't hard to identify the former taxman's gifts and previous calling. He speaks more about money than the other writers. For example, where Mark, Luke and John reference mites, farthings and pennies in their gospels, Matthew speaks of talents and pounds in addition to the other kinds mentioned by the other three. He also employs terms that aren't found in the writings of the others – tribute, piece-of-money, gold, silver and brass. He employs terminology that clearly indicates his familiarity with finances – debts, reckoning and money changers.

The Holy Spirit didn't cancel out the humanity or the backgrounds of the gospel writers, but expressed Himself through them. He does exactly the same through us.

From the pulpit, our first and foremost responsibility is to exegete the Scriptures and teach people the Word of God. But as we do this, we inevitably share our experiences and tell our stories to illustrate and put flesh on the text we are seeking to unpack. The divine treasure flows through an earthly vessel and it seems, to my constant amazement, that God is not ashamed of my flesh; instead He wants to weave it into His ongoing story. As we relate our experiences and tell our stories, people come to understand what we are passionate about and committed to. The stories we tell, reveal our hearts. Your stories of faith, risk and even – perhaps most of all – failure, are the things that will shape your cultural environment.

You may feel uncomfortable about pushing your personal stories into the limelight. Of course, it is possible to step into the spotlight in an illegitimate manner, but false humility isn't any less ugly than inordinate pride. It's important to see your life stories as a resource – a gift from God – for communication.

God outfits Himself in flesh. As unique and vital as the Incarnation was and is, it wasn't – in one sense – a one-off event. He continues to clothe himself in flesh – ours. We are incarnations, with a small 'i.'

We have all heard the noble but misguided prayer of the budding preacher, 'Oh God, make me invisible, so that people will see you.' God's plan doesn't include making us invisible, rather, He intends that people see and experience His treasure through earthen vessels.

How does this work in practice? If you desire, for example, to create a culture in which people are released to take risks of faith, then tell of your risky ventures of faith. Make risk-taking and mistakes a feature of the stories you tell. This gives people permission to enter into that story themselves, makes the proposition more realistic and makes them feel less alone in their experiences. Then tell, or have them tell, their own stories.

How you shape and tell a story is crucial in creating culture.

Let me give you an example of a story that I have told many times at our current church, Gateway, and how I tell it so as to shape a particular outcome.

A number of years ago, I was on my way home from the church office. We lived in a rural area and I was enjoying the leisurely drive through the picturesque Waikato countryside. As I came up to a blind corner, the car following me pulled out and overtook me in an extremely dangerous manoeuvre. The shock of the driver's stupidity, and then the relief at the fact that there was no oncoming traffic, caused me to spontaneously shout out a somewhat irreligious exclamation.

In the midst of my unspiritual moment a sudden, unexpected thought flashed through my mind: 'That car is stolen.'

It stunned me to the point that I questioned its origin.

'Lord is that you?'

As the car raced off into the distance I took note of its registration number. KH2020. Arriving home shortly afterwards, I went straight to the telephone and called the police. It wasn't that I was certain I had a stolen vehicle to report but rather an insatiable curiosity to know where the thought had come from. I fumbled to explain to the answering officer that I thought I might have just encountered a stolen vehicle – minus the 'God possibility' of course.

The policeman seemed singularly unimpressed with my detective work but, moved I suspect by a sense of duty, he agreed to check the computer for any recently reported stolen vehicles. Suddenly he was back on the line with a completely different disposition. With a sense of urgency he said, 'That car *has* been stolen sir. Where was the driver heading?'

I told him the general direction and approximately how long it would take to arrive at the outskirts of the next town. He quickly thanked me and hung up. I was ecstatic. I had heard God's voice! That seemingly rogue thought wasn't just a figment of my overheated desire for justice or some Freudian wish fulfilment to see dangerous drivers get their comeuppance. It was the Lord.

Later that afternoon, I received a phone call from an officer based in the small town where the car was headed. He introduced himself and thanked me for my assistance. Then he informed me that they had apprehended the driver of the stolen vehicle, and asked the question I was dreading, 'Mr Barry, could you tell me how you knew that car was stolen?'

I replied, 'Officer, I don't think you would believe me if I told you,' hoping that this would somehow put him off pursuing the question.

'My pen is poised Mr Barry; please tell me.'

I gulped and then attempted to explain the inexplicable.

At the end of my muddled discourse there was a long silence from his end of the phone. Just when I was beginning to imagine that the line might have somehow become disconnected, I heard a slight shuffling noise and then a timid voice said, 'OK, thank you Mr Barry. Goodbye.' Click.

Now, I could tell that story in a manner that might lead listeners to be (mistakenly) impressed with my spiritual sensitivity. I could say that as the car overtook me, God spoke to me in a deep baritone voice that resembled Charlton Heston's, and told me that the vehicle was stolen. In hindsight, it seems He did exactly that, minus the baritone voice, but at the time I wasn't at all sure it was the voice of God.

When I tell this story I usually labour the point that many of us have thoughts like this one and tend to dismiss them as the vagaries of our own thought processes. But in fact, these kinds of thoughts can originate from the Holy Spirit. Frederick Buechner beautifully describes this inspiration as, 'thoughts that I did not choose to think, chose me to think them.'[9]

In telling a story like this, I am seeking to create an atmosphere or culture in which it is permissible to tentatively follow through on these kinds of thoughts and see if they really have originated with God. People who dogmatically assert that God spoke, 'Charlton Heston-like,' to them over some issue, tend to scare and intimidate us all. We might be impressed by them, but we rarely think we can imitate them. I much prefer a more cautious approach that acknowledges the level of uncertainty that we – or at least I – tend to feel in these moments. I want to allow for the possibility that I have heard wrongly – something that has happened numerous times as I have tried to learn how to identify that inner voice. I think this approach is within the reach of nearly all of us. This we can imitate. My story thus told helps to create a culture in which permission is given to experiment. It fashions an atmosphere of expectation and faith, and an ethos in which failure is an acceptable part of learning.

In our shared life as a church community, there will be stories that become part of our corporate folk lore. We tell and retell these stories. The retelling serves to remind us of God's faithfulness to us and reinforces our shared value system.

A third significant factor in engineering your environment is how you, as a leader, react to critical incidents and organisational crises. Powerful cultural signals are sent out to others by what you as a leader react to, or do not react to. Your reactions reveal your underlying assumptions and values.

Ecclesiastes 3:8 states that there is 'a time of war and a time of peace.' Wise leaders discern the seasons and know when to pick up their weapons and when to refrain.

You must choose wisely the moments to go to war for what we believe are the purposes of God.

As desirable as it might be to have a setting in which there are no wars that need to be fought, such a setting doesn't exist this side of heaven. Leaders are warriors. Times of war require commitment, resolve, energy, strategy and significant amounts of time. These are the very same things that create culture. This being the case, it is imperative that we battle for the right issues.

An astute leader knows that not all battles should be fought. Some hills aren't worth a frontal assault. A wise old Quaker once quipped, 'You can't die on every cross.'

Some leaders fight for everything and, as a result, end up more pugilist than pastor. They box and bully their way through life, and the only culture they create is toxic with issues of control and animosity.

On the other hand, some leaders won't go to war over anything. At the sight of battle they run for safety. Let me be blunt. If you aren't willing, as a leader, to put your life on the line over key issues, then you have no business shepherding God's flock. Sometimes a shepherd has to face down bears and lions.

What you are willing to fight for helps establish your cultural values.

Early on in our time at Gateway we faced a situation that I believed was crucial for setting the direction for how ministry was to be carried out among us.

At an Annual General Meeting of the congregation (remember those things?) it was noted that pastoral visitation wasn't being done to the satisfaction of some within the congregation. It was suggested from the floor that additional staff should be hired to take up the slack.

I'm afraid I rose to the bait like a blue marlin, and a

battle royal ensued. I explained that ministry shouldn't be handed off to so-called professionals. Ministry was the task of the whole Body of Christ, and to hire staff to do the work we were all supposed to be engaged in was, in my view, completely unacceptable. People needed to be visited, but not by professionals. They needed the caring contact of fellow members of the church. I didn't want to see the development of a clergy/laity distinction when it came to ministry within our congregation.

In the discussion that followed, I argued that this idea, while perhaps sincere, was seriously misguided and should not be acted on. The congregation grasped the strength of my feelings and I think saw the logic of the argument.

I noted with concern, however, that a number of the existing staff members were shaken and confused by the discussions of the evening and seemed unsure of how they should cast their votes. The following week, in our staff gathering, I took the time to explain my reasons for entering into this battle.

In their presence, I felt freer to make the strength of my feelings known in a manner that would have been inappropriate in the public setting. To their shock, I explained that had the remit on hiring pastoral staff passed, they would have needed to find a new pastor. I would not allow ministry to be confined to professionals, and felt so strongly about the issue that I would have rather resigned than pastor a church that headed in that direction. I needed my fellow church workers to understand the strength of my convictions.

The 'war' I engaged in let the staff and the people know how important this value was to me.

Wars of this intensity are rare; in fact I could count on one hand the number of times I have acted this strongly in 20 years of ministry at Gateway. It remains the only time in my entire ministry when I have publicly (and even then only to staff) threatened to resign. Some issues are vital in terms of long-term ramifications. There are hills worth fighting over and, in some cases, dying for.

Choose your wars well, for they will shape the corporate environment for better or worse.

Another means by which we shape our environmental culture is to be intentionally aware of the 'recompense system' of church life.

Edgar Schein comments, 'Leaders can quickly get across their own priorities, values and assumptions by consistently linking rewards… to the behaviour they are concerned with.'[10]

I'm not speaking primarily in financial terms, of course (although that is not to be totally discounted either, for how you allocate financial resources and set budgets clearly reveals your assumptions and beliefs).

By 'recompense' I'm referring to what we highlight, what we publicise, what we invest in, the kind of leadership we advance.

Steven Kerr, the Chief Learning Officer at General Electric once wrote a famous paper that he entitled, 'The Folly of Rewarding *A* while Hoping for *B*.'

He observed that there was 'often an inconsistency between behaviour that leaders desired in people and the reward system that the same leader had put in place; for example rewarding individual performance while hoping for teamwork.'[11]

If we, as leaders, are intentionally trying to build a particular culture, then we must ensure that the 'reward system' of our organisation is consistent with our values. Although the message is initially conveyed by the behaviour of the leader, it will be sustained in the long-term only if the important rewards are consistent with that ongoing behaviour.

It is so easy, as pastors and leaders, to spend all our time with people who are doing the wrong things. We spend hours with them trying to straighten them out. The more they sinned, the more they disobeyed God, the more time and energy they get from us. Meanwhile, the people who were doing the kinds of things we longed to see, for the most part, get ignored. Pastorally, we tend to oil the squeaky wheel.

Without deliberately meaning to, we essentially recompense waywardness. I know that dysfunctional issues and people need to be dealt with and spoken to, and that time – sometimes significant time – must be spent in bringing healing. However this needs to be intentionally balanced with giving our time to the things we want to see reproduced in our churches. What we give our time to sends a powerful message regarding what we think is important.

A significant part of leadership, and of building a healthy culture, is ensuring we are recompensing the things that we want to see more of.

When it comes to placing people in key roles within the church, a profound question to ask is, 'How many more people like them do we want in the church?'

If the answer is 'none', then we have committed the folly of rewarding A while hoping to get B. Remember, leaders reproduce after their own kind. There have been occasions when we, as leaders, have been guilty of advancing people into key positions to keep them, or others, satisfied and quiet (or for some other equally illegitimate purpose). We invariably pay a greater price further down the road because of our unwillingness to pay the cost of the unpleasant task of upsetting people in the short-term.

The word pictures you paint are an incredibly powerful force in creating culture. In his master-work *Poetics* (330BC), Aristotle famously stated, 'The most important thing is to have command of metaphor.'

A metaphor is a non-literal figure of speech in which a word or phrase is used to enhance the meaning and description of another object or idea.

Powerful metaphors have the capacity to redefine and reinvent how we perceive reality. In his book *Viral*, Leonard Sweet comments,

> When you rearrange images in people's minds, you are doing brain surgery and, by extension, life surgery. Jesus' ministry can be seen as metaphor surgery, which is soul surgery. He replaced one way of looking at God and the world with new mental models... Our thoughts can be held prisoner by a long established image, and

when that image is reframed or changed the chains are broken.[12]

The power of metaphors came home to me when I was considering how I could change a wrong way of thinking about a group of people who were attending our church. The group in question was university students. Gateway is located in a university city, and each year new students scope out our church, remain with us for the duration of their studies, and then move on.

What disturbed me was the way I heard some of our leaders speaking about these students: 'Students! You can't *build* anything on them. They come, draw off our resources and then head off into the ether, leaving us without anything substantial having been built.'

As I thought about how I could expose what I saw as our deeply flawed assumptions, certain metaphors used by Daniel Brown in his book, *The Other Side of Pastoral Ministry*, were particularly helpful. Brown speaks of churches being either lakes or rivers.[13]

In some ways, lakes and rivers are similar – both are essentially made up of the same substance, water. Both can be beautiful and both can provide hours of fun for swimmers and boaties alike.

But in other crucial ways, they are very different.

Lakes don't go anywhere. They are essentially static. There is little or no current. When you swim in a lake, you enter and exit at the same spot. The only thing a lake can do is get larger or smaller. Depending on the season, the intensity of the drought or amount of rain, it shrinks or becomes enlarged.

A lot of thinking about church, it seems to me, is 'lake thinking.' Leaders are often primarily – if not exclusively – concerned with the issue of shrinking or expanding. We give no thought to the issue of 'current.' In Gateway's context, because of our 'lake' mentality, students became annoying. They got in the water and then, three years later, they left. They swelled the numbers and then had the temerity to leave and make our growth statistics look poorer. 'We can't build anything on them.'

The problem was we weren't thinking about transporting them anywhere.

Ultimately, the flaw in our way of thinking lay in the fact that rather than *serving* this group of people we were seeking to *use* them.

It seemed that we didn't exist for them but rather vice versa. Rather than seeing students as nuisance value – here today gone tomorrow, and leaving nothing substantial behind – I began to talk about the privilege we had in having these impressionable lives for three crucial years of their development.

This is where the river metaphor came in. A river can do many things a lake cannot. Primary among them is the ability to move and transport people. A river has current. Swimmers who venture into a river know that they won't get out at the same place they got in. The river will take them somewhere. When I spoke, I began to paint a picture of us trying to take these students somewhere while they were in the Gateway River.

We existed for them, not vice versa.

Whenever a new student began attending our church, we had three wonderful, potential-filled years in which to transport this young life towards becoming a man or woman of God.

The crucial issue was not *how many* people we managed to cram into the lake, but rather how far our river could take them; not how many swimmers there were, but what was happening with each swimmer.

As we developed this metaphor, there were other aspects of it that we were able to highlight. Rivers have banks that direct their flow. I likened these banks to our corporate value system – our culture. If a river breaks its banks, it is no longer productive; it is a destructive flood. If we broke through our value system, then the results would ultimately be destructive to all concerned.

The metaphor of the river became a powerful force that directed Gateway's thinking and behaviour and shaped our corporate culture – a fact certainly helped by the ever-present image of the Waikato River, which flows through our city.

Well-constructed, appropriate and relevant metaphors can do what pages of argument struggle to achieve. It isn't without reason that the old adage informs us, 'A picture is worth a thousand words.'

Schein comments, 'Leaders do not have a choice about whether or not to communicate. They only have a choice about how much to manage what they communicate.'[14]

As leaders, we are creating culture. If we don't do it with a degree of intentionality then it will occur by default. I propose that one of the chief tasks in our leadership roles is to think clearly about, and be very intentional in, creating culture. An environmental cultural architect paints intentionally and creatively, and it is a privilege for us to fill this role in our churches.

CHAPTER 6

Valuing People

As we grappled with how to build an ethos, a culture that would lead to the release of dreamers and visionaries, I soon realised that the value system we adhered to would be a crucial element in the process. Identifying our core values was a process that took a number of years. Finally they became clear as they emerged from our journey and from our study of the Scriptures.

The first basic core value that undergirds our ministry is that we choose to value people.

This may seem like an utterly obvious or trivial point. But on reflection, I think all of us are aware of situations in church life when people weren't valued. Rather, as was the case for our university students at Gateway, they were treated as resources to be used rather than persons to be served.

I believe that God's supreme passion is people. He wants relationships with people. Jesus died for people. The church is made up of people. In any endeavour that bears His name, people must be loved and served.

As I have taken pains to point out already, we must be so careful lest, in our pursuit of goals, we confuse means and ends.

People are the *ends*, while structure and programming are the *means*. In my early experience of church life, this truth was tragically reversed. We were more interested in how many people attended a programme than we were about whether the programme had served and benefited the people.

Many times the language we use betrays us. For example, a new family arrives at church and we hear through the grapevine that some of its members are gifted musicians. On the way home from the service we say to our spouse, 'I hope they stay, we could sure *use* them!' Again this may seem a trivial observation, but I suspect that on more occasions than we care to admit, the language we use amounts to a Freudian slip.

I remember being in a ministers' meeting at a large church that had just constructed a new sanctuary. One of the senior leaders of the church was commenting on the finances required for such a construction project. 'We need to get some lawyers and doctors saved. We have to pay for this building somehow!' he said. Perhaps he was joking, but I noticed that neither he nor anyone else laughed. In this case, a certain category of people (ones with high income potential) had been crassly reduced to chequebooks and cash.

Jeremiah the prophet has some chilling words for leaders who are tempted to reduce people to so much cannon fodder for the sake of institutional goals.

> Woe to him who builds his house [read 'church'] by unrighteousness and his upper chambers by injustice, who uses his neighbour's service without wages and does not give him his pay… (Jeremiah 22:13 AMP)

The Message version renders this verse, 'Doom to him who builds palaces but bullies people: who makes a fine house but destroys lives.'

Brennan Manning comments, 'Whenever religion shows contempt for or disregards the rights of persons, even under the noblest of pretexts, it draws away from the reality of God.'[1]

When Caiaphas, the High Priest, declared that it was needful for Jesus to die for the sake of the nation and the temple, his religion had left the realm of respect and love for people (John 18:14). His concerns were motivated by the need to keep the religious institution functioning at an optimal level. It was the procedures of religion – the temple, the institution, the structures, the abstractions – that he cared for, and he was willing to allow an innocent man to die in order to obtain and sustain them. From my observations, I think that the spirit of Caiaphas is painfully alive and well in the church at large today.

One of the nuances in the way this value for people is worked out in the church context of which Karen and I are a part, has to do with the refusal to control or manipulate the people we lead. It probably doesn't require an astute psychologist to note that our sensitivity to this nuance comes from our experiences under Dave's leadership. But my observations and interactions over the 30-plus years since would lead me to believe that controlling leaders are fairly commonplace.

Sometimes the desire to control may be crass and raw, born out of insecurity. In other situations it may appear in a far more sophisticated manner, and can even be rooted in a genuine desire for another's well-being. Whatever motivates it

– the noble or the ignoble – manipulation rarely ends up being healthy for either the one being controlled or the controller. Eugene Kennedy suggests, 'the devil dwells in the urge to control rather than to liberate the human soul.'[2]

Again, Brennan Manning puts it eloquently when he says,

> The fundamental secret of Jesus was his sovereign respect for human liberty. He never tried to make people virtuous against their will. The institutional church is untrue to the law of its own being when it violates freedom. Whenever any authority figure seeks to suppress freedom, he or she is thereby setting themselves (however unconsciously) in opposition to Christ. God created us in his own image because he wanted free, responsible service. Whenever the virtue of obedience is reduced to a pattern of domination and submission, we produce trained cowards rather than Christian persons... If we really knew the God of Jesus we would stop trying to control and manipulate others for their own good, knowing full well that this is not how God works among his people.[3]

Whenever I find myself tempted to minister in a way that removes or weakens a person's capacity to act freely, even if I genuinely believe my actions might be for their benefit, I remind myself of C S Lewis's pungent lines, 'Of all tyrannies, a tyranny sincerely exercised for the good of its victims may be the most oppressive.'[4]

As a leader I have the immense privilege and responsibility

of serving and resourcing others on their spiritual journey, but I do not have the right to choose their path for them or bully them towards what I think is the best direction for that journey.

I can, and will, encourage, exhort and, if necessary, reprove when I see people being self-destructive, but I must do so in a way that allows them the freedom to make their own decisions. People have to live with the consequences of their choices, but I believe they must be free to choose.

This value underpins everything we do, from the way we make announcements to our expectations regarding people's attendance at church services and events.

For example, in making announcements, we *inform* without *promoting*. This leaves people free to decide what their schedule will or won't allow in regard to their attendance, without the associated guilt that occurs when they choose not to come to a meeting or programme that may have otherwise been promoted as an event that should not, or must not, be missed. We avoid those kinds of phrases. I think all of us have been to meetings we were told we couldn't miss, only to realise later that we actually could have missed them, and we wished we had!

In regard to attendance, I make sure people realise they can genuinely choose which events they will attend. I refuse to upbraid them – either directly or indirectly – for that choice. It is inevitable that some people will make poor, lazy and straight out 'carnal' decisions – that's human nature. But I make it clear that they are responsible for their own spiritual development and maturity. I am a shepherd, not a policeman.

I believe that Scripture indicates that people should regularly be part of a community of faith (Hebrews 10:25) and I will teach this unequivocally, but it is not my jurisdiction to determine what 'regularly' looks like in their situation. They must do this for themselves in good conscience before God.

I seek to faithfully serve and shape people in biblical patterns of thought and conduct, but my conviction is that maturity cannot come from imposing external standards.

Hebrews 7:19 states, 'For the Law made nothing perfect, but the bringing in of a better hope did, by which we draw near to God' (MKJV, see also Hebrews 10:1).

According to Paul, the law is holy, just and good (Romans 7:12). The reason the law cannot perfect a person doesn't lie with some fault in the law's adequacy. Rather, the problem lies in the fact that it is an external imposition. Maturity (or as this translation terms it, 'perfection') comes only as we make a heart response of our own volition to what is good, holy and just.

A response achieved through coercion or manipulation using guilt or fear, is not the same as a response born out of inner conviction. We must be vigilant to attend to this value. I am painfully aware how easy it is, especially when frustrated by people's apparent 'slowness' or 'foolishness', to slip into a dominating or controlling mode.

There is a passage from Paul's epistle to the Galatians that keeps me vigilant about seeking control. Galatians 5:20 somewhat surprisingly lists witchcraft as a work of the flesh. When I first noticed this, I was taken aback – I'd always assumed that witchcraft was associated with the work of evil spirits. There is no doubt it can become the domain of dark spiritual forces, but Paul seems to be making clear that witchcraft starts with our own desires.

I believe the essence of witchcraft is an illicit desire for control. In its ultimate form, people seek to use spiritual power to obtain their goals. There's a tendency to imagine that this kind of thing only happens in faraway places. But in its early stages, it is found in forms of behaviour that are frighteningly familiar. Witchcraft as a manifestation of the flesh comes in the form of manipulation, intimidation and domination. Whenever guilt is used to motivate people, as it often is, intentionally or inadvertently, even to apparent godliness, we 'know not what spirit we are of' (Luke 9:55). Using guilt as a motivator is akin to athletes using steroids to enhance their performance. The initial results can be spectacular, but the final outcome is disastrous. It is essential that the methods we use to see the Kingdom come are in keeping with the nature of the Kingdom we represent.

Our goal is that people feel valued and loved in every ministry interaction they have with us. As leaders, we may not see all the people we pray for healed; despite our best efforts, we may not be able to provide all the wisdom people seek in counselling situations; we may not be able to meet their present needs. But it *does* lie within our jurisdiction to love and value people in all these interactions. I'm painfully aware that the actual doesn't always match up to the ideal, but nonetheless, this is the goal we strive for.

Having hit upon the importance of loving people, and avoiding manipulation, Karen and I began to live this value out, as best as we were able, among our little congregation in Cambridge.

But things were about to take a turn that we hadn't envisaged.

CHAPTER 7

Divine Leadings and Nasty Surprises

We had been in the beautiful town of Cambridge for eleven years. We loved life there. The wounds from our previous church experience had healed nicely. We were surrounded by people that we loved, and our congregation was doing well. Our children were happy in their schooling, so there was certainly no desire to move. However, I found myself in an unusual season.

Restlessness seemed to grip me. I would arrive at my office each morning, and within an hour I would be pacing the floor. This was completely out of character for me. I am generally a settled person (I think Karen might call it 'boring!') and would happily work for an entire day without the need for a break. But something had changed. I would try to read the Scriptures but find myself distracted; I would open a book but do no better; I would put on a cassette tape but would inevitably turn it off again, unaware of what I had just listened to. There were numerous days when I would arrive home mid-afternoon, much to Karen's surprise, and go for a run to work out my frustration.

In the middle of this season, I rang a friend for advice. After listening to me for a while, he simply asked, 'Don, do you think God is preparing you to move from Cambridge?'

The idea hadn't occurred to me and I simply said, 'No, I don't think what's happening is about that. What makes you think that might be it?'

John explained that one of his moves had been preceded by the exact same sort of restlessness. He said that when a gardener plans to move a tree or large shrub, they will dig around it and loosen the earth several days before moving it. This allows the shrub to adjust to its changing circumstances, rather than be totally shocked by a sudden move.

I understood what John was saying and was grateful for his advice, but didn't think it was applicable.

I soon changed my mind. Within a four week period following this conversation, I had four invitations to pastor other churches. This had never happened before – it wasn't as if I had been turning down offers every other week for the past ten years!

Karen and I discussed John's comments and we agreed that, at the very least, we should see if God was saying something to us through these invitations and my restlessness. We set aside a one-month period and independently sought the Lord. At the end of the month of dedicated prayer, we both returned empty-handed. Neither of us had any significant leading that the Lord was trying to move us. We decided that, in the absence of any specific guidance, we would stay put. I simply resolved to get over my restlessness and push on.

A week later, I was at a denominational conference. During

a ministry time, as the worship team were singing and people were praying and talking in small groups, I was quietly waiting on the Lord. Suddenly someone tapped me on my right shoulder. I turned to look and was faced by a man I'd never met before. The stranger seemed mildly embarrassed and explained that he thought the Lord had given him a word for me. He simply said that he felt the Lord was about to move me from the church I was in and that my next move would be to a city. The mystery man then quickly walked away and I was left watching him retreat into the distance, wondering if I'd had an encounter with some kind of Lone Ranger.

While I was still turned to the right, in the direction of the man's departure, I was tapped on my left shoulder. I turned again. This time it was a man I did know – one who was regarded as having a credible prophetic ministry.

'Don,' he said, 'this is going to sound strange, but I feel God telling me to tell you that you are to move from Cambridge. You are to move to a city.'

To say that I was stunned would be an understatement! After the conference, I returned to Karen and we discussed what had occurred. There was no way these men were in collusion or that the second man had heard what the first had said. With my mind still reeling, the following week I had another meeting to attend in a neighbouring city. The speaker, an American visitor, was ministering. Truthfully, I don't think I heard a word he said. I was trying to come to terms with what it seemed the Lord was saying. As the preacher concluded his talk, he looked at me and said, 'Are you thinking about leaving your church?' I tried to mumble something as unspecific and incoherent as possible, so as not to give away my thoughts. I succeeded admirably in both departments as I recall.

Then he said, 'Yes, you are supposed to leave the church you are in; you are to move to a city.'

Karen and I were left without doubt that the Lord was about to move us. We knew we were to leave Cambridge, but had no idea what 'city' God had in mind for our final destination.

After working through the issues with the leadership team at the church, we announced our plans to leave. The next few months flew by in a blur. We had several other remarkable confirmations that God was truly in this move. The church was well prepared in terms of its leadership to make the change; in fact it went so smoothly that we left somewhat bemused at how easily and quickly people had adapted to the new person appointed to take our place! I mentioned earlier how certain situations were tailor-made to demonstrate the ever-present, though hopefully retreating, insecurity in my heart!

As news of our impending move from Cambridge hit the denominational grapevine, we had expressions of interest from a couple of city churches. A large church in the neighbouring city asked whether I would be interested in looking at being the pastor there.

I knew quite a bit about this church by virtue of its proximity, and also because the senior pastor, who had recently departed for Australia, had been the superintendent of our movement and an influential figure. The church's culture made me shiver – it was everything we weren't and didn't want to be. The whole situation reminded me too much of our previous disastrous church experience. I must admit that I didn't even pray about the offer. 'No, was all he said!' to quote a line from a song called 'The Weight' by The Band.

Another church, in our capital city, showed some interest and we visited and talked with their leadership team about what they required. Although the idea looked quite promising for a time, the door closed and we were left wondering where this prophesied but elusive city might be.

My friend John, the one who had first suggested that God was moving me on from Cambridge, worked for a mission organisation. He now got in contact to ask if we would be interested in relocating to Singapore to help run a 'finishing school' for missionaries who were about to go out into the field.

Because Karen and I had a deep interest in missions, we were immediately attracted to the idea and registered our enthusiasm. The only problem was that the school was two years away from being up and running. Staying in Cambridge for another two years wasn't an option, so we were left wondering what the interim would hold.

Then the large church in the neighbouring city, which I had previously turned down, came back to us again. This time they asked if we would consider leading their Bible School. We told them about Singapore and offered a two-year deal if they were interested. They were. We quickly found ourselves in charge of Evangel Ministry Training School in Hamilton.

The first few services at our new church did little to allay our fears about its culture and style, but we consoled ourselves with the thought that our position was only temporary. I resolved to stay out of any leadership role in the church itself, turning down their request to be on the elders' oversight team, and determined to confine myself to the activities of the Bible School.

In those first few months, despite my reluctance to be involved in general church life, I was taken aback by the number of people who approached me for counsel regarding sexual brokenness in their lives. I had never encountered anything like it. I think I finally rationalised that what seemed like a disproportionate number of sexual issues was simply the result of the size of the church. With that many people, the number of cases was bound to be higher. Perhaps because I was new, people felt safe with me – encouraged by a sense of anonymity that came with the fact that I knew nothing of their past history. Not long afterwards, I had a disturbing dream. I dreamed that I was driving along a road that had a large, steep bank on the right hand side. As I proceeded down the road, I could see ahead of me a large culvert going into the bank. A man in a white suit, similar to what emergency crews wear when they clean up chemical spills, was going into the culvert with a large rake and was pulling out onto the roadside copious amounts of foul material. I recall being sickened by what was exposed there. Then I awoke.

I knew the dream was significant in some way and determined to explore its implications in the morning. I fell asleep again and had the same dream in what seemed like an exact action replay. The next morning I was pensive and worried. I intuitively knew that the Lord had given me the dream, but at that point I had no idea what He was saying to me, except that it obviously had to do with revealing some form of uncleanness.

Whose though? I had no idea.

I was, as I recall, hoping God wasn't saying something about my own life – I wasn't aware of anything, but I didn't discount the possibility. The fact that the dream was repeated intrigued me. I remembered that in the story of Joseph it is recorded that the Pharaoh had a dream that was given to him twice. I opened my Bible, intrigued to read, 'The repetition of your dream means that the matter is fixed by God and that he will make it happen in the near future' (Genesis 41:32 GNT).

My daily readings in the Scriptures that first morning after the dream emphasised purity of heart, and I came away convinced that the Lord was about to do or say something significant on this issue.

Two days later, I was in my office at the church, preparing for lectures at the Bible School. My thoughts were interrupted by a knock at the door and I looked up to see a staff member standing there looking very pale. I invited her to sit down and asked how I might help.

She blurted out, 'Oh God, Don, I have just had a woman come into my office and confess to having had an adulterous affair with...' and she named the previous, well known, highly regarded pastor of the church. The content of my dream flooded back and I sat there stunned.

'Are you sure the woman is being truthful?' I asked incredulously.

'Without doubt,' she replied.

This incident set off what I can only describe as a divine set up of dominoes that tumbled over, one after another. Within a two-week period, we were made aware of at least four other women who had also been involved with the same man. It happened without us probing or investigating. They bubbled to the surface as if divinely compelled to tell their stories at the same time, quite unaware of each other.

In the midst of this unravelling, I had another dream. In it I was standing in a field looking at an old wooden house some distance away. Suddenly, in a series of jumps, I was close to the house, looking at one of its old wooden-framed windows. It was peppered with small holes that indicated some termite-like creature had been busy at work for many years. A hand suddenly appeared, like something from Belshazzar's feast (Daniel 5:5). In the hand was a flame that moved close to the surface of the timber. The flame disturbed the creatures within the wood and they came tumbling out of the window frame, seeking to escape the heat.

The morning after this dream I was again in my office, when another staff member knocked and entered. He slumped down into a chair, looked at me and said, 'We have just had another woman come and confess to adultery with...' And yet another revelation about the same pastor was made. The staff member put his hands on his head and added, 'This stuff is coming out of the woodwork!'

Touché.

I knew without a shadow of doubt that this was the Lord's doing. It was His divine hand and flame that was exposing what had occurred. I needed, and was thankful for, the assurance that the dream had given me. It strengthened me. When we took the shocking news to the appropriate church authorities, we weren't exactly met with open arms.

The first port of call was to talk to the person who was the current senior pastor of the church. He was a 'spiritual son' of the man in question and the thought of exposing his mentor was equivalent to the sin of patricide for him. Somewhat understandably, he vacillated and considered for a moment, pushing the news back down into the sewer from whence it had appeared to come. Ultimately, good sense, including his own, prevailed and we took the news to the movement's executive team.

It goes without saying that they weren't exactly overjoyed with the news we brought. I suspect we were viewed like a cat that has dumped its night-kill on the doorstep. There was a flurry of activity as the executive contacted their Australian counterparts to discuss the situation, and hopefully hand the issue over to them. The logic was that since the offending pastor was now ministering in Australia, he lay within their jurisdiction.

The Australians passed the issue back to New Zealand – the logic being that since the issues occurred on the New Zealand executive's watch and in their territory, it was their responsibility to deal with. The executive discussed handing it back to us – the 'logic' (if you can call it that by this stage) being that the whole episode was perhaps a demonically inspired attempt to bring down a reputable pastor and sully the good name of a godly movement!

Maybe, some said, the mess should be buried and we should speak of it no more. There was, however, far too much evidence of wrongdoing for this option to be seriously contemplated, and there were too many people of integrity at all levels to allow the voices of a fearful few to hold sway. The situation went public.

CHAPTER 8

Sexual Failure in Ministry

I'll pick up the main thread of our story again shortly, but I need to pause for the moment to focus on a subject I would much rather not have to address at all. The issue needs to be addressed, not least of all because, in my experience, it is alarmingly common.

Observing and being part of the subsequent 'clean-up' of a trusted leader's significant sexual failure is a sobering event.

It has made me think a lot about the need to finish well. It seems, from my personal observation and historical study, that many people who start in ministry with idealism and exhilaration don't breast the tape running as strongly as when they started; if they finish at all.

As noted at the beginning of this book, Karen and I came into the things of God, and soon after into ministry, during an era that we now call the Jesus Movement. Beginning on the West Coast of the USA in the late 1960s, the Jesus Movement swept across the world bringing thousands of young people into a new and vital relationship with Jesus. We found ourselves, like so many others, caught up in the thrill of this newfound relationship, and, like so many, felt a call to give our lives to serving God.

We poured over the 'trench parapets' into ministry and spiritual warfare with youthful innocence and naivety. And we fell in that field in vast numbers – wounded, or forever turning our backs on what we once believed. Some who survived were left with a corrosive cynicism that has haunted them ever since. Many, if not most, of our friends and acquaintances who entered into ministry around the time Karen and I did, are no longer in Christian service; and a significant number of them would no longer even consider themselves Christians.

Dr Robert Clinton, Professor of Leadership at Fuller Theological Seminary, has engaged in extensive study of leaders and leadership, both biblically and post-biblically. His findings are sobering, if not downright upsetting. He claims, 'Few leaders finish well. Of those on which information was available, less than 30 percent finished well.'[1]

In other words, two out of three leaders either didn't finish the ministry task at all, or finished it poorly.

We don't have to go far in the biblical record to find leaders who started well but finished poorly. Among the more well-known are characters that we have already mentioned in this book: Saul, Solomon and Judas.

Saul was 'an impressive young man without equal among the Israelites – a head taller than any of the others' (1 Samuel 2:9). He began with an imposing series of victories that made hope soar and the future look bright for the fledgling nation of Israel. A short 42 years later, Saul is a wizened shadow of the man he once was. Victories have been replaced by defeat, and hope has given way to despair. Saul had resorted to the occult for guidance and died by his own hand on the battlefield.

Solomon's name became synonymous with wisdom, and yet his last years weren't exactly stellar. He forsook the wise counsel of his younger days and followed after the 'strange women' that he had warned other young men about in his book of Proverbs. A great start degenerated into a pathetic end.

In the New Testament, Judas Iscariot is perhaps the most tragic figure of all. Called to be with Jesus along with 11 other hand-picked contemporaries, for three and a half years he had the privilege of an incomparable 'Bible school' experience.

After a promising start, which included preaching the gospel, healing the sick, casting out demons and being party to Jesus' many displays of power, Judas became increasingly addicted to the lure of financial gain. As the treasurer of the small band of followers, he had unprecedented access to the corporate purse and took that opportunity to amass significant personal wealth, which included a property portfolio purchased with the 'wages of unrighteousness' (Acts 1:18).

Today, instead of ranking alongside Peter the Rock and John the Beloved in a hall of fame with the other apostles, his name is synonymous with treachery. A promising start, a damnable ending.

If even the Apostle Paul was concerned lest he be 'shipwrecked' and not finish his course (1 Corinthians 9:27), then I think it wise that we carefully consider what is required to complete our journey.

The reasons for not finishing the course are as many and varied as the runners themselves, but there are certain factors that recur. By paying attention to these pitfalls, we can be more diligent to avoid them.

Robert Clinton lists seven major barriers to finishing well: the failure to function with integrity in the use of finances; the abuse of power; inordinate pride that leads to downfall; illicit sexual relationships; family failures; plateauing (by which he means a failure to keep growing and learning); and psychological wounding.

Old-timers in the Pentecostal stream used to talk of 'Girls, Gold and Glory' as being the three great hindrances to a ministry finishing well.

In my circle of colleagues and associates, it has been the 'girls' component of that old adage that has cut the widest swathe through our ranks. Sexual failure has, it seems, reached almost epidemic proportions among people in ministry. It's this threat to finishing well that I wish to focus on for the remainder of this chapter.

I don't think it requires huge insight to see that the overt, and almost complete, sexualisation of our culture over the last several decades has normalised illicit sexual activity.

Pornography in print, motion media and electronic forms has increased exponentially. What would have horrified our parents, is now standard fare for Hollywood and Madison Avenue. Behaviour that would once have been considered shameful, and perhaps even illegal, is now exhibited with pride, lauded as daring, courageous and authentic.

The idea of restricting sex to marriage is now considered odd, quaint and unlikely.

People who enter ministry aren't immune from the blatant sexualisation of society. Many enter ministry with their own sexual history and brokenness that can create fault lines or points of weakness in their character.

The danger is further compounded by the very nature of pastoral ministry itself which, rather than protecting us from sexual failure as we might have expected, may in actual fact set us up for it.

The church provides a context in which men and women can work together on projects. Because of personal faith, passion and giftedness, these projects lie close to the hearts of the participants. The shared intimacy that arises from participating in a common, heartfelt cause can, and often does, serve as a catalyst for the development of sexual attraction between a leader and a colleague of the opposite sex – or, it has to be said, of the same sex.

The intimacy of shared work is both a wonder and a potential terror. Peter Rutter, in his book *Sex in the Forbidden Zone*, comments,

> When two people work together in a context where familiarity and trust develop, they may experience closeness in each other's presence. Because sexual intercourse is a symbol for our deepest intimacy, a deepening sense of intimacy with another can arouse sexual desire.[2]

I suspect that the stakes are raised even higher in churches where spiritual passion is embraced. In contexts where emotional responses are opened up and encouraged, emotions can sometimes spill over into the sexual realm.

It has been well recorded in church history that times of great religious fervour have also been times of increased sexual failure. Historians have noted how the camp meetings of the American frontier were, without doubt, an effective tool in evangelising and civilising the settlers. Yet these emotionally charged events also, it is noted, heightened passions for something other than piety. Observers cynically noted that, 'as many souls were conceived as were converted.'

In her book *Who Walk Alone,* the missionary teacher Margaret Evening remarks about the phenomenon observed by missionaries of a higher incidence of sexual immorality following religious revivals. She comments,

> Fervent prayers and worship often heightens our awareness and longing for love in all directions and not only God-ward. It [spiritual fervour] not only expresses love, it engenders it as well.[3]

Researchers who have studied the neurochemical processes of the human brain have noted that the passion leading to spiritual fervour and the passion leading to sexual activity stem from the same kind of physiological chemistry. Though occurring in distinct but parallel channels, spirituality and sexuality are separated by a wall thin enough for osmosis to occur. The impulses can get switched, and people's love for God can be transferred into romantic feelings for another, such as a leader who represents godly warmth and acceptance.

Obviously I'm not suggesting that we shouldn't be involved in shared projects, or that we should somehow try and damp down spiritual passion and limit expressive worship. I'm simply suggesting that we need to be alert and attentive to circumstances that represent the potential for relational thin ice and keep an eye out for early warning signs of a developing emotional attachment.

Leadership often involves working under a level of responsibility and stress for longer periods than are healthy. Physical and emotional burnout are significant issues for leaders and take a huge toll. I suspect that burnout is often underestimated as a contributing factor to the poor decisions that lead to sexual failure. People do things when they are exhausted that they would never contemplate when they are rested.

Marine biologists have discovered that pods of whales that beach themselves are often suffering from high stress levels. Some scientists have postulated that this is what drives the animals onto the beach. Beaching may well be the whales' attempt to bring the stressful situation to an end. Many leaders who beach themselves through an illicit affair, have arrived at a place where, in their exhausted and confused thinking, beaching somehow represents an escape. I know of a pastor who discussed with another staff member the possibility of having an affair as a means of getting out of ministry which, at that time, was particularly stressful.

Effective self-care is not the subject of this book, but

suffice to say, we must ensure that we are healthy leaders – emotionally, physically and spiritually. Our level of health may make all the difference when we are faced with crucial decisions.

As counter-intuitive as it sounds, seasons of spiritual success can also create a context for sexual failure. It was, after all, at the height of his success that David fell into the Bathsheba affair.

Dean Ludwig and Clinton Longenecker studied the circumstances of successful business leaders who failed morally. In an article, aptly entitled 'The Bathsheba Syndrome,' they offered four characteristics that were common among these leaders.[4]

Firstly, they noted that personal and organisational success often led these leaders into a place of complacency. The leaders lost their strategic focus and allowed their attention to be diverted to things other than the management of their organisation.

Secondly, it was observed that success often gave a leader privileged access to information, people and objects within the organisation.

Thirdly, this access often led to an unrestrained control of the organisation's resources.

Finally, the researchers noticed that success has the effect of inflating a leader's belief in their present ability to manipulate or control outcomes.

When the loss of strategic focus is combined with privileged access, leaders can succumb to the temptation to use their position and status to promote what Ludwig and Longenecker rather coyly call, 'non-strategic, non-organisational purposes.'

The researchers commented, 'Even an individual with a highly developed moral sense can be challenged by opportunities resulting from the convergence of these four factors.' Such leaders can become 'emotionally expansive, developing an insatiable appetite for further success, thrills, gratification and control.'

One of the costly side-effects of vocational success can be isolation from spouse, family, friends and peers. In these cases, there are also fewer and fewer people prepared to risk challenging the leader's increased expansiveness. A combination of these factors create a potent cocktail for moral failure in the life of the 'successful' leader.

Over the years, I have talked with numerous leaders who have failed sexually. As we discussed the events that led to and flowed from the moral failure, I noticed some recurring patterns that, had they been identified, may have signalled deeper trouble on the horizon.

The first danger signal began when leaders found themselves becoming mentally preoccupied with a given person. This step usually didn't trigger alarm bells since, most often, these early thoughts weren't specifically sexual in nature. This allowed the leaders to continue with the preoccupation unabated, and deceived them into thinking they were on safe ground.

Mild, seemingly innocuous feelings of infatuation didn't seem to pose much of a challenge and, mistakenly, the leaders assumed they were in complete control of the situation.

The second recurring pattern was an unusual desire to spend time with the specific person. This led the leader to manufacture situations that provided contact. As yet, nothing outwardly illegal or illicit seemed to have occurred. Serving on committees together, going out in a group to the movies, or attending an event doesn't have the effect of raising eyebrows. The leader is easily able to justify the behaviour in their own mind.

The third signpost, and one that really should be raising red flags, is finding the opportunity to give frequent compliments to the person. This isn't the same as expressing normal gratitude for work well done – it has moved several steps beyond that.

Provided there is reciprocity in the developing relationship, it can quickly move to the next stage, which is communicating at a much deeper level. Conversations are long and meaningful. Whenever you find yourself sharing matters that you haven't yet shared with your spouse, then you are not on thin ice – you are waist deep in water. A sacrosanct line has been crossed that constitutes 'emotional adultery.' It is giving to another that which solely belongs to your spouse. Unless this situation is quickly acknowledged for what it is and arrested, the chances of it ending in physical adultery are considerable. Physical intimacy is the natural conclusion of emotional intimacy.

Nearly all the leaders I talked to, mentioned that they then began to make comparisons between the person they were preoccupied with and their spouse. These weren't, at least at first, sexual comparisons. The primary points of focus were attitudes, ways of relating, levels of respect and perhaps things like their dress sense or even personal hygiene. 'She never nags me; she is always pleasant and seems to really appreciate the sacrifices I make. She is always dressed so smartly. My spouse slops around in track pants and is always on my case, and I never seem to be able to please her.'

Soon after the comparisons, sinister logic is often set in motion. It goes along the lines of, 'This is such a special relationship. Why has God allowed it at this time in my life? Perhaps He has a plan for it. Is something going to happen to my spouse? Will they have an accident or contract some medical condition? Is God preparing me for my future?'

As extreme as this reasoning sounds in the cold light of day, to those increasingly becoming enmeshed in a demonic snare, it seems reasonable and even possible.

Many leaders made a crucial mistake at this point. They sought to verbally define the relationship with the person they were attracted to. Sometimes this took the form of saying something like, 'This is such a special relationship. We must take precautions to ensure it stays on the right footing.' As righteous as this might sound, it is completely wrong-headed and can be a subtly disguised attempt to ask the question, 'Do you feel the same way I do?'

I know of some who have 'confessed' their feelings to the person they were attracted to, asking forgiveness. All it takes is a reciprocal confession and an accelerant has been added to the smouldering fire.

The final pattern I noted in each case, was the unwillingness of the leader to hear the warnings of others who were, by now, starting to see signs of the attachment. In every situation, the leader thought he or she was in complete control.

It has been observed by people who work with fallen leaders that, almost without exception, these leaders assert that they could have terminated their entanglements at any time. They portray a sense of omnipotence. They seem to totally underestimate the power of attachment needs and emotional forces, and they completely overestimate their power to disengage and disentangle themselves.

Finishing well is by no means a given. Those who manage it, do so by virtue of the cultivation of a holy vigilance. I don't mean to engender a sense of paranoia, causing you to think that every normal, healthy relationship is a potential minefield. Then again, perhaps our naivety hasn't served us well. Perhaps we need to be aware that every relationship has potential pitfalls given certain circumstances.

What happens when failure occurs? What happens when the horse has bolted? There will be those who say, 'I wish I had heard all this stuff earlier, but now it's too late for me. I've failed. Is there any word of hope for me?'

Of course there is. Our God is a redeemer – a redeemer who takes broken things and restores them. He does it in any field of brokenness we care to name, including in the area of moral failure. You can be restored. But it will certainly take time, patience and forgiveness.

I think people often mistakenly assume that forgiveness

and trust are one and the same thing. God ministers forgiveness when people repent, and we mistakenly conclude that since God has forgiven the fallen minister, we should too. Our forgiveness will then be demonstrated by the rapid reinstatement of the guilty party.

As a result of this kind of misguided thinking, I have watched ministers announce a moral failure, take a break which is sometimes measured in days or weeks, and then be quickly restored to the pulpit by fellow leaders who say things like, 'Your ministry is too valuable to be shelved for a failure of which we are all capable. Let him who is without sin cast the first stone.'

But public ministry is based around trust and credibility – not just forgiveness. While it is true that forgiveness can be ministered immediately after genuine repentance, trust can not. Trust must be earned, and when it has been damaged by moral failure there must be a season in which it is conscientiously rebuilt. This time will be measured in years and not in months.

There is always the possibility of restoration, but the process must be managed wisely and well by others, and not simply by the fallen person themselves. Thankfully, there are wonderful stories of wise and well-managed restoration

Sexual failure need not be the final word. While failed ministries grab headlines and seem to throw the shadow of suspicion far and wide, I am incredibly glad that many people in public ministry run the race well. They are the unnoticed faithful and deserve praise and thanks for a job well done.

CHAPTER 9

THE FALLOUT

When the news was finally made public about the former senior pastor's moral failures in Hamilton, the impact on the local congregation was catastrophic. Anger, disillusionment, betrayal, denial and accusations that the man of God had been shafted, swirled around the atmosphere like a toxic nuclear cloud.

The letter of confession and apology, when it finally arrived from the offending pastor, was so vague in its content and weak in its confession that it simply created more difficulties. Those who believed he was innocent felt they were justified in their view, since he clearly had not confessed to the things of which he had been accused. Those who believed the reports, were outraged at the trivialisation of his sins and the damage he had caused. The church went into free-fall.

The pressure and confusion seemed unrelenting, and our senior leader stumbled emotionally under the weight of events. He became indecisive regarding his continued leadership of the church at a time when the church so badly needed decisive leadership. The confusion and insecurity among the staff was palpable. One by one, they made their way to my office and poured out their concerns. In effect, each said the same thing, 'I can't carry on like this, I'm thinking of leaving.'

I asked each in turn if they had talked to their pastor and, ascertaining that they hadn't, sent them off with that assignment. I would then turn and think wistfully of Singapore; it was becoming more like paradise every day. The end of the two years couldn't come soon enough. I wanted out.

One weekend, Karen and I were ministering at a pastors' conference in another city. We returned home to the news that in our absence, and without our knowledge, the staff had got together in discussions and had sent a delegation to the senior pastor. They virtually demanded that he make up his mind as to whether he was going or staying, giving him two weeks to decide. The environment of uncertainty had become untenable. The sting in the tail of their ultimatum was a fateful addendum which stated that if he was staying, then they, to a man and to a woman, would leave.

Understandably, he left, and he was bleeding profusely. When the news leaked regarding the staff's actions, about 80 to 100 people in the congregation were so outraged they also left. Rumours of a 'colonel's coup' were rife within the church and throughout the wider denomination, and for many, both inside and outside the church, I was perceived to be the colonel.

Karen and I held our tongues and dreamed of Singapore.

For some, the suspicions around my involvement weren't lessened when the church board approached us and asked if we would consider taking the senior leadership role. We had one year left before we were departing for Singapore. The best we could offer was that I would act as an interim leader while they looked for someone else.

The church, understandably, was in a tailspin. The initial shock of pastoral infidelity on a grand scale was now followed by the departure of their current senior leader in less than desirable circumstances. The convergence of these two events contrived to create a perfect storm, which threatened the church's very survival. We were haemorrhaging people. They left in their droves.

At its height, about 1400 people had attended the church. Now, in our darkest days, about three to four hundred were in attendance. I was receiving between three and five resignation letters a week from those who wrote to inform me of their impending departure – most didn't bother to write. On one occasion, some folk informed me that they were leaving, and when I asked if there was a particular reason that I needed to address, they simply replied that they were leaving because so many others were leaving.

Now the church was in a dire financial position. We still had a million dollar mortgage on the building. To my surprise, I was told by the administration staff that we had, for the last while, been operating in the red, and currently had a $40,000 overdraft. There was a cap on our credit limit of $50,000 and we appeared to be missing the budget by between two and five thousand dollars a month. I figured we had about five or six months before we hit the financial wall.

With church numbers dropping dramatically, and the financial situation worsening week by week, we had to take drastic steps in order to survive. We were staffed for a church of a thousand, so it seemed, in the cold light of day, that we needed to reduce the wages bill.

After everything the staff had endured, this seemed like the last straw. We had to lay off half our paid employees. Nearly all those affected accepted the decision in good grace knowing we had no other choice. Most remained in the church and continue to this day as part of the congregation. It is a testimony to their faithfulness and commitment.

About this time, I received a phone call from the mission organisation that we had regarded as our ticket out of all this mayhem and hellishness.

'Don, the plans for the finishing school for missionaries aren't going to happen. We can't pull them together. We're sorry but Singapore is off the table. We're so sorry.'

'Not half as sorry as us, believe you me,' I replied with a sense of nausea overtaking me.

My emotions ranged from shocked disbelief to straight out rage. I felt tricked by some divine sleight of hand and was left wondering how God had managed to conjure up a situation that left us stuck in a role we had so desperately and studiously sought to avoid.

As the initial shock passed and depression set in, I remember quietly contemplating the situation. I thought back to Cambridge and the decisions we'd made as we prepared to leave our previous post. The thought occurred to me that perhaps if I had prayed about the original offer the church had made for us to be senior leaders instead of simply saying a prayerless no, things might have turned out differently. Perhaps I would have still ended up being in the same role, but without so much grief. I didn't, and still don't, have an answer to that question. Meanwhile, our church was a holed ocean liner, and water was coming aboard too quickly for me to sit contemplating counter-factual might-have-beens.

We had a visiting speaker come to the church at this time. In addition to being a pastor, he functioned in the United States as a church growth consultant. He observed our situation and asked if he and his wife could take Karen and me out for a meal. Later, sitting overlooking the beautiful Raglan Harbour, eating the quintessential Kiwi meal of fish and chips, he delivered his blunt but not so surprising conclusion.

'Don, this church is going down.' Then he added, 'I have watched numerous churches go through what you have gone through and I have yet to see one come out the other side. Get out and get out now!'

As realistic as his assessment seemed, it just wasn't an option for us. We were now all in, for better or worse, for richer or poorer, till death (or a revived Singapore) do us part!

We determined that the first thing we needed to address was the church culture, and the process of transformation would need to start with our remaining staff.

We booked a retreat centre and took the team away for a time of assessment and contemplation. On the first morning, I took a whiteboard and stood before them. I explained that I was going to write up some words. What I wanted from them was their gut-level immediate reaction to those words. I didn't want a well thought through theological explanation or some sanitised answer shorn of its emotional content. Assured that there would be no rewards or censure, no right or wrong answers, just whatever-may-come responses, we began.

The first word I wrote up was 'people.'

The responses came more quickly than I could write, but I managed to scribble the following responses: 'keep them,' 'get more,' 'numbers,' 'expendable,' 'merchandise,' 'means to an end,' 'must conform,' and so it went on.

When the responses finally ebbed away, I moved on to the next word: 'worship'.

Once again I scribbled frantically as the staff members got into the swing of it: 'hyped,' 'lacking heart,' 'three fast and three slow,' 'set a platform for what is really important – the preaching,' 'lacking spontaneity.'

'Giving' was the next word on the board.

By this stage, some of the staff were almost on their feet as they shouted their responses: 'give to get,' 'another tithing sermon – sigh,' 'milk it,' 'hidden agendas,' 'manipulate,' 'abuse of visiting speakers.'

I was vividly aware of that last point. Some months previously, we'd had a visiting speaker come to the church for a series of mid-week meetings which I was asked to coordinate. I asked how the finances would be handled and was told to take up an offering each night. Everything that came in would be handed on to the speaker.

I duly took up an offering and was thrilled to be told at the end of the meetings that the people had given generously and that we would be able to give our itinerant speaker a cheque for $10,000. Remembering that this was the mid-1990s, it was a considerable sum. The following day, someone from the financial department came into my office and informed me that they would be passing on $2,000 to the speaker. I registered my surprise as calmly as I could.

'I was told the whole offering would go to the speaker.'

'Yes,' they countered, 'but we didn't imagine that amount would come in. It's way too much money for four days of meetings. We can't give the speaker all that.'

'I informed the congregation each night that all the money that came in would be passed on directly. This is an issue of integrity,' I protested.

'She's not getting that amount of money,' was the firm response.

I summoned up my courage and enquired as to whose responsibility it would be to inform the congregation of this decision. My inquiry was met with a look of incredulity. It was as if I'd gone completely mad. I continued, 'Either you tell the congregation of your decision or I will. I will not be party to stealing from this speaker what rightfully belongs to her.'

The person left the room without another word, and later that day a cheque for the full amount was presented to our guest. I had assumed this was a one-off incident, but when it came up as a whiteboard statement, I realised practices like these were probably more common than I'd thought.

We continued with a number of other words, including 'leadership style,' 'facilities,' and even 'dress code.'

After about 30 minutes of writing, I figured we had enough of a bead on our church culture to have a conversation. I stood back from the board and asked another question. 'This is who we are. Do we like who we are?'

I could never have predicted the response. If I had foreseen the outcome, I might have left well-enough alone. There was a stunned silence as they looked at what I had written, what they had said. The silence at first seemed to deepen as the unmistakable evidence of our toxic culture hit home like a blow to the solar plexus. Then the silence was broken by a person weeping. Someone else started to weep more loudly, and this was joined by another sobbing uncontrollably. The weeping and sobbing spread like a prairie fire over drought-stricken summer grass, and within seconds the whole group was engulfed in some kind of cathartic outpouring.

People fell from their chairs onto the ground; one beat the floor with her fists shouting at the top of her distraught voice, 'You b#@#*d, you b#@#*d!' I assumed, I think correctly, that she wasn't directing her comments at me but at the man she had served for so many years and who had cruelly betrayed her trust by his sexual failures.

I recalled my 'geyser encounter' with Dave. In so many ways it was similar, only on this occasion it was all the more powerful because of its group effect. I was stunned into silence, and simply retreated from the whiteboard to sit on a chair on the outside the circle. At times the outpouring seemed to die down, and then regaining its energy, it would rise, stretching for new heights of emotional release. The emotions seemed to be an explosive cocktail of anger, betrayal, contrition, grief and relief.

After what seemed an interminable time, the room was quiet. People were strewn across the floor, others slumped in their chairs and some standing, disorientated, surveying the carnage.

When people had gathered themselves, finished wiping tear-stained faces, straightening their clothing and comforting one another, I moved back to the whiteboard and erased the damning indictment we had recorded against ourselves. I asked another question, hoping and praying this would result in a more cheerful outcome, 'What would we like it to be?'

'People' was once again the first word up. Once again, slowly at first but quickly becoming machine-gun-like in rapidity they began, but this time there was such lightness, almost a celebratory, musical note to their contributions: 'unique,' 'cherished,' 'free,' 'flourishing,' 'treated with integrity' they shouted out, and on it went until we had filled the board and we sat satiated, with a palpable sense of hope rising in our hearts.

We continued with the other words and by the end of the morning we had completed our task. I spoke about the need for a well defined set of values that would somehow gather up and encompass all we had written and that would guide our corporate journey into the future.

It seemed that without any prompting, the team had arrived at the same set of values that Karen and I had worked out over the previous decade. When I wrote up our values on the whiteboard it was as if they all rose together and with one voice cried, 'Bingo!'

We agreed that valuing people, integrity, authenticity and vulnerability would be our guiding principles, our modus operandi.

Of course, we were all painfully aware that, so far, we had only accomplished the easiest part of the work ahead.

We now had to take our newly defined cultural ideals and put them into skin; we had to incarnate them and make them an actual and accurate description of our culture.

When I told them that this would take between seven and ten years to achieve, they were shocked. 'Surely not! Six to twelve months should be an adequate time,' seemed to be the general consensus.

I explained that you might be able to spin a jet ski on a sixpence, but an ocean liner takes kilometres to be turned around. Culture that has turned toxic cannot be remedied with a quick fix. Change isn't easy and cultural problems can take considerable time to put right.

It would take us years – and not a few tears – to create our new culture.

CHAPTER 10

Confronting the Spirit of Poverty

We left the retreat later that week, cleansed, encouraged and determined that we would see the church rise, phoenix-like from the ashes of shame and failure.

Immediately before us, however, lay the seemingly insurmountable problem of our dire financial position. The burden of servicing our million-dollar-plus mortgage had been obvious even before so many people had left the church. The strain now became unbearable. We were careering towards a financial precipice that threatened to make irrelevant all our best intentions and resolutions to see the church restored.

After prayer and contemplation, I went to the leadership team with a plan. I suggested to them that I needed to preach a series of messages on giving, and that at the end of the series we would take up an offering. The idea was met with the nodding of heads and a murmur of approval. But when I announced the final aspect of the plan, mouths dropped aghast, and the nods of approval were replaced with the shaking of heads in disbelief.

'We are then going to give the offering away,' I said.

I was faced with stunned silence. Inquiring eyes asked, 'Are you completely mad?'

Slumped, resigned shoulders seemed to pose the unspoken question, 'First we get an adulterer and now we get an idiot?'

Somewhat reluctantly, and perhaps with an air of fatalism, they finally agreed to the plan.

That Sunday, I shared with our diminished congregation the plan to solve our financial crisis and, to my great surprise, they all applauded wildly when I announced we would give the offering away.

As I contemplated this response later, I could only conclude that the congregation were either more faith-filled and wiser in the ways of God than we supposed leaders were, or they were cheering in anticipation of a colosseum-like circus in which blood was going to be shed in a spectacular and unforgettable manner – like the excitement of looking at a car crash. I now know it was the former.

With the teaching series on giving duly completed, we took up the offering and it amounted to about $25,000. Had we kept it, it would have been sufficient to halve our overdraft and guarantee us at least an extra 12 months of operational life. We resisted that temptation and gave it to a struggling orphanage in Tajikistan.

For the next few months, the regular giving stabilised enough to keep our noses slightly above the rising water line of debt repayment.

Three months later, there was a knock on my office door. Our financial director, David, stepped into the room and informed me that a lawyer had just called him with some news. Up until this point in my limited tenure, nearly all the news I had received had been of the kind you would prefer not to have been given, so I braced myself internally, and enquired as to what a lawyer might want with us.

David looked at me with the traces of a grin forming and said, 'A woman who used to be part of this congregation three decades ago has died and left us $160,000 in her will.'

I suspect, in hindsight, I will always feel mildly guilty for the inappropriate response I made to the news of this poor woman's passing. 'Thank you Jesus!' I shouted. 'I mean, I'm sorry to hear about the lady, but ... thank you Jesus!'

I tried to rephrase my response several times, attempting to make it more appropriate in some way, but each attempt simply served to dig a deeper and, for David, more amusing hole. Finally I decided to give up and obey the 'first law of holes': when in one, stop digging! We simply rejoiced in God's goodness and for the woman's generosity.

God's miraculous provision put us back in the black at the bank for the first time in several years. It was a wonderful first sign for us of God's intention to work His redeeming grace into our brokenness and shame.

This incident has become one of Gateway's seminal stories.

It has had a profound influence on the way we think about our resources, financial and otherwise.

When we are in a place of privation, the natural tendency is to hold tight to the little we have and scramble to find more.

We readily acquiesce to what many have termed 'a spirit of poverty.' To refer to poverty as a spirit might seem strange to some; 'I thought poverty was a condition. What do you mean by a *spirit* of poverty?'

I don't think we can restrict and relegate poverty to a

simple condition of *not having*. I think it goes beyond that to grip us with a *fear* of not having. It goes beyond material reality into the abstract world of emotion and belief. When we view poverty in this way, it is easy to see how a spirit of poverty is not simply the jurisdiction of people who are struggling financially. It can, and does, affect every strata of society. Even ridiculously wealthy people can find their lives bound by this spirit.

The spirit of poverty causes people to hoard and be tight-fisted.

I heard a wonderful story once about a group of orphans who had been rescued from the streets. They were placed in a caring orphanage where, for the first time, they had regular sustenance. Instead of eating out of trash cans they went to bed with full stomachs. For the first time in their lives, these children had adults that cared for them, comforted them and protected them. But, despite the improvement in their fortunes, they cried themselves to sleep each night.

The volunteers at the orphanage were at their wits' end to explain and remedy the situation. Then, in a flash of insight, one of the workers suggested that perhaps the children were fretful not because they were hungry, but because they were afraid of what tomorrow might hold for them. Nothing in their brief and bitter experience of life to this point had given them any reason to expect consistency. Yes they were well fed today, but tomorrow might change all that.

As a result of this insight, the workers came up with a new bedtime ritual. Every evening, as they tucked the children up for the night, each child was given a large bread roll that they could hold or stow away under their pillow. The crying ceased. The assurance that there was provision for tomorrow calmed the children's fears.

The power of fear works to undercut any impulse towards generosity. The spirit of poverty resigns us to not having and as a result we resolve not to give.

There is a passage in the Book of Deuteronomy that describes precisely the impact that this spirit has on our lives.

> If there is among you a poor man of one of your brothers inside any of your gates in your land which the LORD your God gives you, you shall not *harden your heart* nor *shut your hand* from your poor brother. But you shall open your hand wide to him, and shall surely lend him enough for his need, that which he lacks. Beware that there is not *a thought in your wicked heart*, saying, The seventh year, the year of release, is at hand, and your *eye may be evil* against your poor brother, and you give him nothing. And he may cry to the LORD against you, and it is sin to you (Deuteronomy 15:7-9 MKJV, emphasis added).

There are four things in this passage that highlight the machinations of a spirit of poverty.

Firstly, there is a 'thought in your heart.' Jesus, speaking to His disciples about not being apprehensive regarding the demands of tomorrow warns them six times not to take thought for what might lie ahead (Matthew 6:25-34). It's the thought that says, 'Don't give that. You can't afford it. You might need that in the days ahead. If you give it you won't have what you need.'

Secondly, when our thought patterns are in keeping with the reasoning of a spirit of poverty, our hearts inevitably begin to harden. Compassion dries up and we rationalise our need to withhold aid to our needy neighbour by virtue of our hypothetical future needs.

As a consequence, thirdly, we clench our fists. We refuse to be generous. We hoard our resources against a rainy day.

Fourthly, poverty narrows, blurs and darkens our vision and we end up with what is described as an 'evil eye.' This phrase is used in the Bible to describe a stinginess of spirit.

Proverbs 28:22 says, 'He that hastens to be rich has an evil eye, and considers not that poverty shall come upon him' (MKJV).

How ironic that the very thing this person is seeking to avoid ambushes him nonetheless. Withholding our resources doesn't deliver us *from* poverty, it delivers us *to* poverty.

Proverbs 11:24 states, 'There is that scattereth, and yet increaseth; and there is that withholdeth more than is meet, but it tendeth to poverty' (KJV).

While this was a lesson that, at Gateway, initially involved finances, I think we learned that its implications went far beyond monetary concerns.

The spirit of poverty has the capacity to entwine itself around many dimensions of our lives and leadership. We don't always recognise it because it doesn't always look like out and out financial greediness.

It can affect the way we deal with all resources. For example,

I am often asked by other leaders about the resources and books I've used as source material for particular sermons I've preached. I am ashamed to admit that my first, instinctive reaction can be to withhold rather than share. 'What if they find out that book or those resources are really good? They might be able to cobble together a series better than mine. I might not seem to be the original thinker they imagine me to be.'

Assessed in the cold light of day, these thoughts are poverty stricken; and yet in the murky moment when the thought is being offered, it seems justifiable to respond with a refusal and a tight fist. I have determined that whenever I encounter that thought, I will respond in exactly the opposite spirit. Instead of hardening my heart, I will respond with tenderness, an open hand, and cultivate what the Scripture calls a 'bountiful eye.'

Proverbs 22:9 says, 'He who has a bountiful eye shall be blessed; for he gives of his bread to the poor' (MKJV).

The spirit of poverty can entwine itself around the way we view and deal with people. We can become precious and protective, not willing that members of our congregation attend other fellowships lest they are tempted to leave ours. I have watched pastors become manipulative as they sought to dissuade people from taking jobs that would move them out of the locality and necessitate attending another church. The methods can vary from mild disapproval to a bullying personal 'prophecy.'

The key to dismantling the spirit of poverty in the financial realm also functions in other areas as well. The spirit is overcome by the commitment to respond to the thought of poverty by acting in the opposite spirit. When we are tempted to close our fist around our resources, we should instead deliberately open our hands and offer generosity.

Our Father is the most generous person in the universe and it is His desire that His children reflect His own nature.

I believe generosity should be a radical and outstanding feature of His church.

CHAPTER 11

The Value of Integrity

One of the values we settled on at Gateway was a determination to walk in integrity in every aspect of our corporate life, and once again this had a particular application in the area of finances.

It is one thing to make a commitment like this in the rarefied atmosphere of a retreat setting, it is quite another when you are down in the trenches of church life.

The remaining staff showed varying levels of enthusiasm and commitment to the new values. A long-term member of the secretarial staff entered my office one day shortly after our retreat and asked me if I still wanted the letters to be sent out to those who had put a large gift in the offering on the previous Sunday.

Mystified by the details of the question, and not knowing anything about these letters, I asked her to explain. I was somewhat taken aback as she rolled her eyes and gave a weary sigh and then proceeded to inform me that there had been an official policy to send letters of acknowledgement, thanks and encouragement to large donors.

I fixed my attention on her and asked, 'Brenda (not her real name), what do you think Jesus might have been hinting at when he said, "Don't let your left hand know what your right hand is doing?"'

Perhaps Brenda was simply wearied and overwhelmed by the changes that had taken place, or perhaps she had concluded that all this values stuff was too much hassle. She put her hands on her hips and shot back, 'I don't know what He meant! Do you want the letters to go out or don't you?'

I concluded that this wasn't an opportune time for a sit-down talk of a serious nature. I simply answered, 'No,' and made a note in my calendar for a future appointment. The meeting never came about; Brenda resigned shortly afterwards and joined the still outgoing tide.

Others of the staff rose to the task magnificently. One morning I was sitting in my office and became aware of a conversation in the reception area adjacent to mine. The secretary's voice, while calm and kind, took on a no-nonsense tone of resolve.

'I am sorry that you feel that way, sir, but I am not permitted by law to give information like that over the phone.' The person was seeking to obtain somebody else's private details. A tense silence followed as this sir responded in obvious anger at being frustrated by a 'mere' secretary.

'Yes sir, I am aware that you are a large donor,' answered Christina, 'however that does not permit you to ask for and expect information that is not lawful for me to give you.'

Another pregnant silence as the caller said his piece. By now I had come out into the reception area, my curiosity piqued.

As I stood beside her, Christina finished the conversation by saying firmly, 'I am sorry you feel that way and you are welcome to take your tithes to another church. What you are not welcome to do is think that your tithes give you the right to break the law. You are not doing us a favour by giving us your tithes, you are simply being obedient to God. We are not dependent on your tithes and we will not allow you to threaten or manipulate us because you are wealthy.' She put the phone down and looked towards me, perhaps wondering if she still had a job.

I smiled, patted her on the back, said, 'You little beauty! Well done,' and walked back into my office.

Living by values may be costly, in this case literally so, but it is always deeply fulfilling and satisfying to know there are things in your life that are not for sale. We had started on the long road of living and functioning out of a well defined and agreed-on value set.

Those first years in the church were a call and challenge to hold up the value of, and function in, integrity of heart.

My thinking and understanding about integrity has been dramatically shaped by interactions with Pastor Jack Hayford, firstly through his tape ministry and more latterly through my attendance at his School of Pastoral Nurture. I can't help but recognise Pastor Hayford's fingerprints all over my thoughts on integrity. I think if I were to be honest, most of this chapter (anecdotes aside) should be in quote marks. I want to acknowledge my gratitude and thanks for how he has influenced me.

When most people think of integrity, I suspect their first

thought is about honesty. Integrity includes honesty, but it is considerably more than that. Honesty is simply an offshoot or fruit of integrity.

In its underlying meaning, the word integrity has to do with wholeness.

The mathematical term 'integer' is a related word (known as a 'cognate' in linguistics) denoting a whole number as opposed to a fraction. Another cognate word is 'integrate,' which has to do with the amalgamation or joining together of disparate elements. An antonym is 'disintegrate,' which indicates breaking something into pieces.

A heart of integrity towards God is a heart that is *wholly* set on God. It doesn't indicate flawless perfection, but rather a complete, unified desire to walk before God in a manner pleasing to Him.

I think this is what the Psalmist was asking for when he prayed, 'Unite my heart to fear thy name' (Psalm 86:11 KJV).

If I were to ask, 'What is the foundational, indispensable requirement of leadership?' I'm sure the answers would be many and varied. Most, I suspect, would be related to the abilities that are so obviously required to lead well – relational intelligence, people skills, administrative capacity, prophetic insight or communication skills. The list is as endless as the conferences and seminars that promise to equip leaders.

But how many conferences have you seen advertised that offer to whet your integrity levels, and how well attended would they be if there were any? Nonetheless, my conviction is that integrity of heart is the foundational requirement for godly leadership.

Of David, the 'man after God's own heart,' it was recorded that God 'chose David also his servant, and took him from the sheepfolds: From following the ewes great with young he brought him to feed Jacob his people, and Israel his inheritance. So he fed them according to the *integrity of his heart; and guided them by the skillfulness of his hands*' (Psalm 78:70-72 KJV, emphasis added).

David obviously possessed a level of natural and practised ability, as indicated by the phrase, 'skilfulness of hands,' but this is preceded both in the order of the words and in the importance of the concepts by another phrase – 'integrity of heart.'

Church history, ancient and modern, has been marred and blighted by leaders who have had skilfulness of hands without integrity of heart. They have illuminated the sky for a season with their charisma and brilliance, only to disappear almost as quickly as they arose, amidst swirling rumours of infidelity, financial irregularity or relational abusiveness.

In 1 Kings 9:4-5, God promised Solomon permanence in his leadership position if he would learn to function with the same integrity of heart as David. Solomon started well but finished poorly. As his heart became divided and disintegrated by his pursuit of foreign wives, he progressively lost grip of the Kingdom of Israel, culminating in it being divided in half and taken from his family – the outer geographical and political divisions reflecting an inner moral and spiritual division.

Proverbs 2:21 states, 'For the upright *shall dwell* in the land

and the man of integrity, blameless and complete in God's sight, *shall remain* in it' (AMP, emphasis added).

The promises of God's word to those who function in integrity of heart are substantial and significant. Consider this passage among many that outline the benefits of integrity:

> The integrity of the upright shall guide them: but the perverseness of transgressors shall destroy them. Riches profit not in the day of wrath: but righteousness delivereth from death. The righteousness of the perfect shall direct his way: but the wicked shall fall by his own wickedness. The righteousness of the upright shall deliver them: but transgressors shall be taken in their own naughtiness (Proverbs 11:3-6 KJV).

Twice in this passage, guidance is promised to the one who will function in integrity: 'shall guide...' (v3) and 'shall direct...' (v6).

The Hebrew word translated as integrity is *tom* or *tummah*. A closely related word, *tummiym*, is the term used to describe the items found in the breastplate of the High Priest – the Urim and the Thummim (for example, Exodus 28:30). We are never given a description of the Urim and the Thummim in the Scriptures but we do know they were used to obtain guidance from the Lord.

The priest carried the Urim and the Thummim over his heart in the breastplate, and he would go before the Lord seeking direction. In some mysterious way the 'integrities' (the literal meaning of Thummim) would give him the guidance he sought.

Drawing from Ephesians 4:30, Jack Hayford describes integrity of heart as 'walking in the power of an ungrieved Spirit.' It is the willingness to take our hearts before God and have Him comment on our attitudes, aspirations and ambitions; to allow him to search our hearts, and see if there be any displeasing way in them (Psalm 139:23-24).

Colossians 3:15 puts it this way, 'And let the peace of God rule in your hearts, to which you also are called in one body, and be thankful.' The peace of God acts as an umpire or arbitrator, guiding our hearts in God's way, speaking to us when there is an infraction that requires correction.

Perhaps another way of framing this would be to say that integrity of heart is the willingness to walk wholly and responsively in the light of an enlightened and Spirit-prompted conscience (Romans 9:1, AMP).

I find it fascinating that the meaning of the word Urim, the second of the objects that were used to discern the will of God, is 'lights.' Integrity requires a willingness to walk in the light.

If we are willing to be available and responsive to the Lord in the small corners of our lives, in matters of honesty, purity and speech, in areas that no one but He sees, then I believe this opens us up to hear God in the larger, more crucial aspects of our decision-making. It is presumptuous to refuse to listen to the internal arbitrator in small matters and expect that God will direct and guide us in larger matters. To be totally available and responsive in small, seemingly insignificant matters is to posture our hearts to hear in the larger matters as well.

Judas Iscariot faced a crucial decision: would he betray Jesus to the religious authorities for monetary reward? It was a decision that would impact his future and eternal destiny.

There is a school of thought that suggests Judas was appointed by eternal purposes to be the betrayer – that he merely played a set role in the divine plan. Therefore what choice did he ultimately have? Andrew Lloyd Webber, in his musical *Jesus Christ Superstar*, grappled with this exact issue. Did Judas have the ability to freely choose to betray Jesus or was he an unfortunate pawn in a much bigger drama? Webber seems to opt for the latter option and has Judas sing a poignant song in which he accuses God of murdering him. He sings,

> I've been used
> And you knew
> All the time
> God I'll never ever know
> Why you chose me for your crime
> Your foul bloody crime
> You have murdered me!
> You have murdered me![1]

I see it somewhat differently. I would also argue that Judas wasn't free to choose other than he did, but not because of some divine impulsion and predetermined plan. Rather, his course was set because of powerful forces that he had allowed to flow in his own life through his lack of integrity.

We know from John 12:6 that Judas was a thief. He had been making wrong choices in regard to money for at least three years, and probably longer. Acts 1:18 tells us that he had bought a field with 'the wages of iniquity.' This wasn't a reference to the betrayal money; he had returned that and thrown it at the religious leaders' feet. This is evidence that he had stolen enough money over the three years of Jesus' public ministry to buy himself a plot of land.

On many occasions he had ignored the voice of his conscience – ignored the internal umpire that had raised its objection to the infraction – and had walked roughshod over godly values in his pursuit of monetary gain. Now, in facing the decision about betraying Jesus for 30 pieces of silver, he is helplessly caught in a flow of his own demise. He is reaping what he has sown.

We cannot ignore God with impunity in small, seemingly insignificant matters and somehow expect that the habitual patterns we have established will be reversed when we come to large, vitally important matters and decisions. Integrity, or its lack, will guide us through all situations – big or small.

Let's look again at our passage in Proverbs 11. These words not only promise guidance through integrity, but also protection and deliverance.

> The integrity of the upright shall guide them: but the perverseness of transgressors shall destroy them. Riches

> profit not in the day of wrath: but righteousness *delivereth from death.* The righteousness of the perfect shall direct his way: but the wicked shall fall by his own wickedness. The righteousness of the upright *shall deliver them:* but transgressors shall be taken in their own naughtiness (Proverbs 11:3-6 KJV, emphasis added).

In Psalm 25:21 David prayed, 'Let integrity and uprightness preserve me.' If we walk in the light of a Holy Spirit-prompted and enlightened conscience, then the shadows that provide cover for the enemy will be removed.

Charles Spurgeon once commented that 'the enemy finds his greatest weapons against us in the stockpile of our own disobediences.'

Genesis 20 contains a remarkable story that illustrates the protecting and delivering power of integrity.

Abraham and his family move to Gerar. Fearful of the locals, Abraham suggests that Sarah lies regarding her relationship with him. 'Say you are my sister. That way, when they see your beauty and desire you, they won't see me as an obstacle to be removed.'

Just as Abraham feared, Sarah's beauty was noticed and she was added to King Abimelech's harem. But before Abimelech could come to Sarah, he was warned by God in a dream about the truth of the situation. Abimelech protests his innocence, 'In the integrity of my heart and innocency of my hands have I done this' (v5).

> And God said unto him in a dream, Yea, I know that thou

> didst this in the integrity of thy heart; for I also withheld thee from sinning against me: therefore suffered I thee not to touch her (v6 KJV).

It is Abimelech's integrity that opens the way for divine intervention and deliverance from what would have been a disastrous and destructive situation.

Ironically, in this incident it is not the man of the covenant (Abraham) that displays integrity, it is the outsider. Abimelech walks with integrity in the limited light that he has, and because of that genuineness, God intervenes.

Another aspect of the blessings associated with integrity seemed particularly relevant to us at Gateway as we pursued our new set of values.

Proverbs 20:7 states that, 'The righteous man walks in his integrity; His children are blessed after him.'

We had seen first-hand how impure and faulty leadership could negatively impact a congregation. Here, it seemed, was the alternative. Not only does functioning in integrity of heart leave a legacy for your natural children, it leaves a positive legacy for your spiritual children as well.

We were keenly aware of the importance of integrity, and were determined to make it one of the undergirding values of our lives and of the church we were now leading.

CHAPTER 12

More Nasty Surprises

I had hoped that the stormy season of nasty surprises concerning pastoral moral failure might give way to calmer waters. It wasn't to be. The integrity we had espoused as one of our foundational values was about to be put to the test in a manner I could never have predicted.

One morning, I was approached by a staff member accompanied by a well-respected member of the congregation who had previously served in an eldership role. The staff person got straight to the point, 'This gentleman has something to say to you.'

I gave the man my full attention and was shocked and sickened by his story. He began by mentioning the name of a pastor.

'This man stayed in my home while he was ministering in this city a number of years ago. While he lived under my roof he sexually molested my two sons.' He explained how this knowledge had emerged and requested that I would take the information to the relevant church authorities.

With a sinking feeling in my stomach, I promised I would.

Several days later, I spoke to a group of executive members from the movement we were part of about what I had been told.

They listened quietly and were genuinely shocked and concerned about the information I presented. They promised that the matter would be taken up with the wider executive body. I left the meeting, somewhat relieved that I had at least fulfilled my commitment to the distraught father and had passed on the information to the right people. The ball was now in their court.

In the weeks that followed, the difficulties we were still dealing with at Gateway occupied my focus, but on occasions my mind would wander back to these latest revelations. A number of months passed and I was genuinely puzzled that we had heard no more from the executive. I began to feel increasingly uncomfortable about having nothing to say to the father who had confided in me.

Opening my mail one morning, I was shocked to find that the particular pastor in question had been invited to be the main speaker at our denominational conference that year. I assumed the executive body must have investigated the claims and found no evidence for the alleged offences. It saddened me that I hadn't been told.

Several years passed, and with their passing, the incident faded from memory. Nothing more was said.

For a week each year, for four years in a row, I attended Jack Hayford's School of Pastoral Nurture at the Church on the Way in Van Nuys, California. Along with about 40 other pastors, this was an opportunity to spend time in consultation with a genuinely godly and wise man.

In 2000 another New Zealander was also part of the consultation, and he was a long-serving executive member of our denomination. During lunch one day, he made a comment that revealed that the matter I had raised several years ago had gone no further than the three executive members I had shared it with. He knew nothing of the incident. To say I was shaken would be a gross understatement. I knew I needed to raise the issue again and enlighten him.

I was astounded that the three executive members had apparently made a decision not to divulge the allegations to the wider governing body of our movement.

In the same week that this conversation was taking place in Los Angeles, something happened in our home church in Hamilton that blasted the issue out of hibernation and into the spotlight once again.

Some weeks earlier, a young man had started attending Gateway. We had been made aware that he had a history of sexually abusing young boys. With the support of his counsellor, he indicated that his desire was to make a fresh start and he wanted to be able to attend the services at our church. We approved on the condition that, while on site, he would be accompanied by a discreet minder. That agreed upon, the young man had been attending for some weeks without incident.

On this particular Sunday, while I was away in LA, the young man deliberately and calculatingly gave his minder the slip and engaged in an inappropriate conversation with another young man in the church. He wasn't far into this conversation when the conscientious minder tracked him down and, ascertaining what was happening, attempted without fanfare, to escort him from the property.

The young man retaliated by protesting loudly, employing a considerable amount of inappropriate language. As the removal was being affected, the man's counsellor, who was also a member of the church, came running to his aid. He was offended by the actions of the minder and loudly announced to everyone that the church leadership had double standards. 'They are heavy-handed with the weak and powerless but they allow the famous and powerful off scot-free for the same crime!' he yelled angrily.

Karen managed to extract herself from a ministry situation and helped quieten the angry counsellor. She assured him that I would hear his concerns when I got back.

I returned home two days later, still with a mix of indignation and profound sadness about how our movement had handled the allegations of sexual misconduct. Karen informed me of the counsellor's outburst and I made contact with him immediately.

As we sat together, I asked him to elaborate on what he had said at church. At first he seemed hesitant and maintained that he preferred to let the matter rest without further comment. But I pressed him, suggesting it was inappropriate to go silent after making such public charges. He thought for a while and then agreed to talk about what he had meant by his accusation of double standards.

It emerged that he was counselling two men who had been sexually molested by the very same person I had so recently been speaking about to the executive member in Los Angeles. It turned out that the counsellor himself had also been one of those affected.

The timing of these fresh revelations seemed too precise for mere coincidence, and I took it as a sign that I needed to follow the issue further and with greater determination.

I asked if I could talk to the two men being counselled. I was subsequently able to have those heart-wrenching conversations, establish the truth of the claims, and observe firsthand the damage that had occurred as a result of the abuse.

Anxious to do the right thing, I asked the men if they wanted to lay legal charges against the perpetrator. They were reticent about the whole issue being dredged up, with all its accompanying pain, and decided against the idea. I contemplated talking to the police myself but I didn't want my actions to be perceived by the men as another betrayal by a church leader. They had made their feelings clear about avoiding the legal system and I couldn't bring myself to go against their wishes.

I made an appointment with the executive member I had been with in LA and shared the original story of abuse, then added the more recent allegations.

He seemed both shocked and distressed, and promised to take the information to the ruling body.

This took place in January. By June there was still no word in reply. The machinery of large organisations grinds slowly, but this delay seemed excessive. I made a decision to phone each of the executive members to ascertain where they were in their deliberations on the issue. I quickly discovered that the issue had still not been tabled. Some members knew of the allegations and others were completely in the dark.

Rightly or wrongly, I concluded that the information

was once again being suppressed and, rightly or wrongly, I determined that I would take action that guaranteed the entire executive were in the know. I wrote to each member individually and laid out the abuse claims as I had received them. This seemed to have the desired effect, and a delegation was dispatched to discuss the situation.

The meeting duly took place at our church and the allegations were outlined again. While the atmosphere was amicable and conciliatory, I was surprised and unnerved when, as the meeting concluded, we were asked what action we thought should be taken. What would 'satisfy' us?

It's easy to jump to the wrong conclusions in such a setting and perhaps I mistook the motivation for the question, but it seemed to have some troubling undertones. I didn't require 'satisfaction.' This wasn't about what was necessary to keep us happy and silent; it was about doing the right thing for the victims and the offender. I was hoping, as the meeting broke up and we went our separate ways, that this wouldn't be simply viewed as an exercise in keeping the squeaky wheel oiled and quiet.

Thankfully, actions were taken following our meeting. Once again the Australian executive body was contacted since this offender, like the previous one, was now ministering in their jurisdiction. The man was approached and he acknowledged that the alleged incidents had indeed taken place.

We were later informed that the offender had already been stood down from his position in Australia pending another incident that was being investigated there. He had taken 'extended leave'.

There are key moments in any story when a certain turn in events irrevocably changes the direction of the plot. Imagine our shock and disappointment when we were finally contacted and informed that it had been decided that the best course of action was to maintain the public stance that the offender had vacated his ministry position for 'health reasons.' Looking from the outside, it seemed that there had been a determined decision to close ranks and not make the findings public – either to the wider community or indeed to the churches and leaders that belonged to the movement.

At first I consoled myself with the argument that I had done all I could. It was no longer my responsibility. But the more I gave the matter thought, the more I felt that my response was completely inadequate.

At the risk of seeming like a dog who refuses to let go of a bone, I once again wrote to the executive registering my disapproval.

At one level, I did understand their motives. The offender was now an elderly man and the idea of public exposure seemed heartless for him and his family. The executive also felt, mistakenly in my view, that it would be better for the movement not to have to face the humiliation of dealing with this sexual failure in a public forum.

In contrast, I felt it was incumbent upon us to view the situation from the point of view of the victims. I suspected they would find cold comfort in the empathy that was being extended to the man and his family. We had certainly not shown those who had suffered most anything like the same sympathy and support.

Having been betrayed once by a representative of the church when the offending had occurred, they were now likely to feel abused a second time.

I entreated the executive to revisit their decision. At the very least, I asked them to be transparent before the members of our movement. This request was met with a refusal. It was felt that enough had been done to bring closure to the matter.

One of my staff had discovered a book entitled *Whistleblower*. It was the harrowing tale of several women who were training to be clergy in the Anglican Church in New Zealand. They were exploited sexually by a person responsible for their training. When they sought to expose the perpetrator, they were met with the same institutional reluctance; the stonewalling, the sympathy for the perpetrator rather than the victims and, above all, the desire to protect the church's reputation in the public realm.

The parallels with what we had experienced were unmistakable and so I, probably presumptuously, took the liberty to buy a copy for each of the executive members. I believed that the situation might yet be dealt with in a way that would befit a Christian organisation.

Two of the seven members of the executive body acknowledged receipt of the book and promised to read it; from the rest, simply silence.

The year was ticking by, and it was once again time for our national conference. Pastors and delegates gathered from all over New Zealand. On the first evening, the speaker – an

American who I presume had no knowledge of what had transpired – spoke about the need to deal correctly with sexual defilement in ministry. The member of the executive whom I had raised the issue with in Los Angeles, and who had always been very supportive of me, took me aside and informed me that a special meeting of the executive members had been called in response to the speaker's message.

'It is my hope,' he said 'that this issue with Pastor _____ will finally be dealt with appropriately. Pray that it goes well. I'll meet you in the morning and tell you the outcome.'

This was a marvellous turn of events. The American speaker's unexpected but precise exhortation had seemingly hit its mark. It seemed that all the prayers and letter-writing might be finally about to yield some fruit.

The next morning I met my friend at the designated spot and time. On his approach we locked eyes and he dropped his shoulders and simply shook his head. 'Nothing more is going to happen, Don,' he sighed. 'They feel that the matter should be left as it is.'

I expressed my frustration at what seemed to me to be insensitive foolishness against both common sense and a clear prompting of the Holy Spirit through our speaker. I left the conference early without attending any of the subsequent sessions.

As I contemplated the outcome while driving home, a thought and course of action galvanised within me. I would not – I could not – continue to be part of a movement that refused to deal openly and transparently with the sexual failure of its leaders. I felt our church's key value of integrity had been breached. I wasn't sure what the members of our congregation might think, or what action they might decide upon once they knew the full story, but I decided that if they wanted to stay in the movement, I could not remain as their pastor.

Our leadership team were unanimous that we should put the matter before the congregation and allow them to determine our future course. I decided that I wouldn't make known my resolve to leave the movement lest it affect, one way or the other, the church's decision regarding the outcome. A congregational meeting was scheduled.

In my last letter to the executive members I had suggested that dealing with the matter publicly, however difficult, was the best course of action. If we were to learn anything from history, especially the history of sexual failure among the clergy of the Roman Catholic Church, it was that transparency was the only thing the wider public would regard as acceptable. The failure of the priests was exacerbated by the unwillingness of the hierarchy to deal with the problems they knew existed. The first failure is tragic; the second unconscionable.

The fact that there are bad apples in every barrel is a truism that needs little in the way of further comment. In every sector of society we see evidence of the fact that people are deeply flawed. The problem is that leaders, who carry responsibility for the overall health of the barrel, often fail to respond with open acknowledgement of, and repentance for, the presence of decay. This issue is even more problematic in the church context, where it represents a fundamental betrayal of the Christian gospel. The gospel always begins with a humble attitude and a heartfelt acknowledgement of failure.

It is incongruous when leaders cause a Christian body to embark on a pathway that they would never counsel an individual to take. Faced with moral failure at an individual level, the counsel would most likely be, 'Unreservedly repent, acknowledge your failure and, where possible, make amends and seek reconciliation. Humble yourself under the mighty hand of God and the way of forgiveness will be opened up to you.'

But, in a turn that defies logic, at a corporate level, instead of embodying the repentance that would be expected from an individual, Christian leaders respond to failure within the wider denominational movement with flight and denial – excusing the apparent sleight of hand by suggesting it is best for the movement.

In the view of the unbelieving public, I suspect that this reeks of hypocrisy and creates a barrier to belief that is virtually insurmountable.

I suggested that the likelihood of information being leaked to the media was something the executive must take into consideration. While I understood something of their actions and desire to protect the name of our movement, I suggested to them that should this go public, their reticence in dealing with the failure might have the exact effect they were seeking so assiduously to avoid.

Imagine my shock and horror, to come back into my

office late on a Friday afternoon to find my somewhat paled secretary with two phone messages in her hand. One was from a television reporter with the *60 Minutes* programme and the other from a reporter with *Holmes* – New Zealand's highest ranked prime-time television current affairs programme.

'Don,' my secretary said in an almost whisper, 'they want to talk to you about Pastor _____. Someone has informed them that there has been a cover-up and they want your comments.'

Many years later, I learned that it was an irate member of our church staff who had contacted these media organisations. An abuse victim himself, he was angered by the executive's seeming resistance, and so took it on himself to force their hand.

My head spun and I determined to vacate the office as fast as possible lest they phone again. I had been the bearer of information to the executive and had pursued a right resolution, but I had no desire to speak to the media at this time. I imagined that the coming of the weekend would be a welcome buffer that might allow some heat to go out of the situation and at least give me time to formulate a response.

I had made the decision to exit the movement and to be truthful. I had entertained the idea of going out as a whistleblower. But my overarching goal was to go in a way that I thought would be pleasing to the Lord. At that point however, I had no idea which option – exiting silently or going out gesticulating wildly – was the pleasing option.

Karen and I discussed the issue at length. In fact, it seemed we discussed little else during those tumultuous times. While both of us were fixed in our decision not to continue with the movement, neither of us was sure how that exit should be managed. Should we talk to the media? What, if anything, should we say?

That evening, after talking and thinking myself into emotional exhaustion, I retired to our bedroom and lay down, my mind spinning. I distractedly picked up the book on my bedside table and opened it to where I had previously concluded reading. It was a book by Warren Bennis called *Why Leaders Can't Lead.*[1] The chapter heading jolted me back to the present. It was titled, 'Quitting on Principle.' The first line read, 'What do you do when the leader is wrong? Not just mistaken or slightly off-base in his judgment, but wrong?'

Bennis talked about the agonising decision of leaving an organisation over issues of integrity. The topic discussed was, should you leave blowing the whistle or simply leave quietly?

I sat upright on the bed, gripped by the relevance of the words on the page. What were the odds of encountering material of this nature exactly at the time when I was contemplating these very questions? It seemed as if the Lord had determined to answer my questions directly and was doing so through this book.

Half way through the chapter, as Bennis discussed the merits of blowing the whistle as opposed to not, I read this sentence...

'Only the producers of *60 Minutes* love a blabbermouth...'

I read and reread that sentence, thinking that my eyes, in my exhaustion, had somehow betrayed me. There in black and white was the answer to my prayer. In the course of the 15 minutes that it took me to read this chapter, I had found the clarity I was seeking. I was to leave, but I wasn't to go as a blabbermouth.

I still wasn't sure how I would handle the reporters, but I determined I wouldn't be speaking to them about the issues. I braced myself for the onslaught that I knew would come. Sexual intrigue is always a winner and never more so than when it involves a Christian celebrity. With a story of this nature, I knew the media would leave no stone unturned.

The first day back in the office, I winced each time the phone rang, but no reporters called. At the end of the day, leaving the office, I concluded that they were obviously doing some follow-up work before they came back to me. Second day; no calls. Third day; silence. By the end of the week still nothing.

I have no idea why the reporters never called back. Perhaps another, more interesting, story broke. To this day, I remain grateful that I didn't have to face the blowtorch of the media's questions, and have rehearsed in my mind how the conversations might have unfolded if I had.

The congregational meeting was duly held and the church, having been informed of the process we had entered into with the leaders of our movement, were as adamant as we were that the course of action chosen by the executive was not acceptable. The vote to leave the movement would have been unanimous except for a long time stalwart who abstained from voting. While he agreed with our position, he tearfully informed me he simply couldn't bring himself to vote for our exit. I understood. After more than two decades as a pastor in the movement, I too was saddened that we had come to this point.

We informed the executive of the decision and I received a curt letter by return mail, expressing their regret at our course of action. They expressed disappointment that we were not able to abide by, and submit to, the decision of the executive body regarding the issue and then added, 'These things [our willingness to submit] are not tested until we disagree.' For a moment I thought of again picking up a pen to express my disapproval and distaste at their sentiments. We had been part of the movement for over 20 years. There had been many occasions when decisions had been made, and courses of action entered into, that I hadn't necessarily agreed with. That's the nature of life in a movement, and I readily accept this. But to suggest that our unwillingness to be part of covering up the actions of a paedophile was an expression of our lack of 'submission' was, to my mind, contemptible. If that was rebellion, then 'rebel' was a label I was willing to wear. In the end, I decided the letters had to stop somewhere and that they might as well stop with me. I laid down my pen; whether in resignation, defeat or simple exhaustion, I'm not sure.

When the news of our church leaving the movement was made public, all kinds of rumours swirled and all manner of accusations were made – mostly by people who had absolutely no knowledge of the lengthy process we had walked through.

Ironically, several months after we left, the executive body reversed their decision and made a public statement to the movement regarding the sexual failure of the prominent pastor. I have no idea what motivated their change of stance. I was subsequently contacted by an executive member who asked whether this decision would, or could, result in a change of mind on our part regarding a possible return to the fold. It didn't.

Too much water had flowed under the bridge and, as Bob Dylan would say, 'too much other stuff too.' Trust and respect had been significantly eroded and we decided that returning was not a healthy option for us. Instead, we determined to continue down our chosen, if unknown, path.

CHAPTER 13

Finding our Redemptive Fingerprint

The value of authenticity had been something I had treasured for many years. Since I was a small child, for some unknown reason, I have always hated pretentiousness. Perhaps it was rooted in the rounds I used to do with my shepherd grandfather.

As we walked, checking on his sheep, we would pass close by the grounds of an exclusive preparatory school for boys. While nothing, as far as I can recall, was ever said that made me feel second class, I was nonetheless distinctly aware that there was a great divide between me and these other boys. Their uniform, their manner of speech and pronunciation, and the expensive sports gear they carried, had no parallel in the world I came from. Who knows, perhaps a child's attempt to somehow redress the perceived imbalance of equity made me decide they were a bunch of fakes.

In the early days of my ministry, my antipathy to white suits and shoes, and the other supposed requirements of a 'truly charismatic' ministry, strengthened my childhood trait. I longed to be truly spiritual and really me at the same time.

I recall listening to a speaker at one of our denominational conferences who suggested that if we wanted to increase our authority in any given situation, a dark suit with a white shirt and tie would help create that effect. Even as a neophyte in the things of God, I recall thinking that if our authority was dependent on the cut and colour of our suits, we were sadly lacking. Suddenly, and probably somewhat childishly, it wasn't just white suits that were a point of loathing and a symbol of a lack of authenticity.

It continued to strike me as strange and sad that when leaders came to the pulpit, they felt the need to be someone other than who they really were. It was as if the anointing somehow turned them into different people, instead of making them a truer, more authentic, version of themselves.

Early in our ministry, a visiting speaker stayed with Karen and me. He was a genuinely pleasant person and I warmed to him immediately. Later that evening, I was stunned when he began to preach. Suddenly he spoke in an American accent, though he was definitely not American. His gestures seemed weirdly incongruous with the man I had encountered in the lounge of our home. His pageantry included taking out a white handkerchief and dramatically mopping his brow, though he wasn't perspiring. The whole experience simply deepened my longing for something authentic for myself and those I led.

The high value we placed on authenticity caused us to encourage spirituality without pretentiousness. In the churches we led, we made it plain that there was no special language required when praying or talking about spirituality. You didn't have to learn some kind of code to show all and sundry that you were acceptable to the 'in group.' We encouraged, and highly valued, *normal*.

No special dress code was required. Beyond a level of sexual appropriateness and, where possible, cleanliness, we had no expectations as to how people should dress. One of my favourite memories is of looking out at people worshipping one Sunday morning and seeing two men standing together, both fully engaged in worship with hands lifted high. One was dressed in a sharp three-piece suit and tie, appropriate for any business meeting. Standing beside him, the other wore old jeans and a black singlet which, in another setting, might have identified him as part of a sheep-shearing gang. Their attire expressed their individual personalities beautifully. They weren't trying to make a statement by how they were dressed; they weren't seeking to impress anyone. Their clothes were simply an authentic expression of who they were. I loved it then and love it now.

At Gateway, we were now at another important juncture in our journey. We were a newly independent congregation, cut off from denominational influences, and we had to make some decisions about church style. Who were we? What would church life look like for us?

There were many apparently successful church models we could imitate. There was a whole range of methods and ways of doing things – from the form worship took, to the preaching style; from the manner in which leadership functioned, to the amount of times and degree of warmth with which newcomers were supposed to be greeted on their journey from the car park to being seated in the sanctuary.

As a pastor, it's hard not to be overwhelmed by the success of the megachurches or movements that invite our imitation.

Sometimes subtly, and sometimes not, they exude the message, 'Be excellent in the same manner and style that we are and you'll enjoy the same success.'

As I mentioned in Chapter 5, I harbour deep reservations about the word 'excellence.' I have come to the conclusion that in many instances, where excellence is being promoted, it faces the real danger of becoming a synonym for 'image'. Image can often be the antithesis of authenticity.

Image is a key product of our contemporary culture. It deals in surface appearance and style. Style has become an end in itself. It is no longer an expression of substance. Today, perception is reality, and identity has become a matter of presentation. I think the famous *Vogue* editor Diana Vreeland summed it up best when she told her staff, 'Never mind the facts, project an image to the public.'

When we watch American presidential campaigning, we cannot help but notice that televised speeches and debates are light on serious discussion and are mostly concerned with the manufacture of the right impressions. Post-debate commentators seem to spend little time evaluating the candidate's ideas since, in truth, there is little to evaluate. Rather, they discuss style and impressions. The debate is won or lost not by the power of the argument, but by the presentation of the candidate: how they looked, used their gaze, smiled, teared up, delivered their one-liners, and displayed their wit.

It is a fascinating and sobering exercise to compare today's political scene with the way previous generations evaluated electoral candidates.

In 1858, Abraham Lincoln and Stephen A Douglas went head to head for the US Presidency. In one particular debate the arrangement was that Douglas would speak first, for one hour. Lincoln would then respond, taking an hour and a half. Then Douglas would rebut Lincoln for another half an hour. This debate was considerably shorter than usual. In some cases, debates lasted seven hours. The ratings for a debate like this today would be low (to say the least).

For the most part, we postmoderns simply aren't interested in substance. As a result of our fascination with style, spin doctors and press agents are more highly valued than research assistants in a candidate's entourage. Postmodern philosopher Stanley Fish quipped, 'Whoever spins best wins the game, make sure it is you.'

Our culture has lost its excellent heroes and has settled for interesting celebrities. We no longer have strong characters, just striking personalities. So many of our celebrities aren't famous for being great, rather they seem great because they are famous. Inner excellence has been exchanged for external image.

Newsweek magazine contained an interesting article that addressed this issue in a powerful and perhaps novel way. It chronicled the rise of plastic surgery. What had started as the attempt to humanely treat wartime injuries, had grown into a multibillion dollar industry, practised chiefly on those in good health, without medical necessity. Only decades ago, such treatment would have been regarded as grossly self-indulgent – if not an actual violation of the Hippocratic Oath.

Newsweek asked the question,

> What lies behind this huge cultural shift in thinking about the place of plastic surgery? One possible suggestion was that over the last century and a half life has changed dramatically from largely rural to overwhelmingly urban. Small, stable, face to face relationships have given way to superficial, largely anonymous acquaintances. The inevitable result is an accompanying shift from an emphasis on internal character to external appearances. In a world in which first impressions may be all there is, plastic surgery becomes a natural resort.

As a play on the facelift phenomenon, the article amusingly but perceptively concluded by asking, 'The underlying question still lurks, are we dragging down character as we lift up everything else?'[1]

My conviction is that what afflicts the individual can also afflict the community – this is certainly true of the church community. In our attempt to make first impressions count, we can concentrate on image at the expense of authentic character. As an example, let's look more closely at a practice I mentioned earlier. I have observed that many churches develop a process by which visitors are ensured a warm welcome on arrival at the church facilities. Greeters are assigned to the car-parking area and their sole responsibility is to shake the hands of all who arrive. More greeters meet you at the concourse and entrance way. Once inside, there are even more extended hands as you are warmly shown towards your seat.

I'm not grumpy enough to have any real objection to such displays of warmth. How could you? It's really rather nice. But my question is, does this process reflect a developing, authentic value within the congregation for personal warmth and love, or does it replace it? If we have developed a process to *express* personal warmth, but not created an *authentic value* of personal warmth among our congregation, then we run the risk of creating an inauthentic environment.

I would sound a warning that if we are going to call people to excellence, we need to be sure we have clearly defined our terms.

In our quest for authenticity, I am aware that others will, and should, influence us. I'm not suggesting that we should try to be impervious to all around us as if we are a diver in a diving bell. A degree of imitation can be normal and healthy, so long as it gives us the tools to find ourselves (our authentic identity), rather than becoming absorbed into a plastic replica.

Authenticity is about finding what a friend of mine calls, 'your redemptive fingerprint.' A redemptive fingerprint is that unique aspect of Kingdom life that you are designed to exemplify. It's that unique thing that you can do best. It occurs when there is a convergence of spiritual gifts, passion and opportunity. Without authenticity, we will end up with thousands of churches that look like second-rate copies of Willow Creek, Saddleback, Hillsong, Bethel and a dozen other replicas in miniature, rather than exhibiting the multifaceted beauty that can only be produced by the authentic expression of Christ's life in every local church.

CHAPTER 14

The Value of Vulnerability

The final value that we embraced which has shaped us both personally and corporately is closely linked with the previous ones. It is the value of vulnerability.

Vulnerability means being honest and transparent about the journey we're on. It's about telling the great stories, but not only the great stories. It's the willingness to disclose the darker parts; the broken regions; the parts that we are tempted to skilfully manage and re-present like a spin doctor might, rather than simply telling the raw, unflattering truth.

Vulnerability wasn't something I was encouraged to embrace in the early days of my ministry. In fact, I recall being at a conference where the speaker exhorted us to opt for the opposite of vulnerability. He encouraged us to remain aloof from the people we led and not disclose or reveal personal information, particularly any personal struggles.

'Don't let them close to you,' he said. 'Let them experience you as a prophet coming out of his chamber to deliver the word of God. Don't show them your clay feet. They will disrespect you and, as a result, will disrespect the word you bring them.'

The rationale seemed to be that if the people became aware of our struggles, our credibility would somehow be diminished. But my experience, even at that early stage of my ministry, has been the exact opposite.

I recall hearing speakers tell their triumphant stories, and admiring them immensely, but I couldn't shake the feeling that my world was vastly removed from theirs. On the other hand, the few speakers I heard that were honest about their struggles, produced both admiration and a sense of relieved identification. Jack Hayford, for example, once shared with a group of pastors about a season of temptation that came close to derailing him in a tragic moral failure. He didn't succumb, and could have easily not mentioned his struggle at all. None of us would have been any the wiser, which is the exact point. His honesty made us wiser.

I'm sure there are some in our congregations that labour under the illusion that we in ministry know little of their pains. I suspect they think that at ordination all links with humanity are somehow magically removed and, from that blessed moment on, we are divinely exempted from the hurt and heartaches that the rest of humanity has to endure.

I think that one of the reasons they have come to this mistaken and distorted perception is that we have often offered such an illusion. None of us mind sharing our minor indiscretions – things that we can laugh about and make us look human. But we hesitate to be vulnerable about the deep and personal struggles we face – the ones that have the capacity to go beyond just making us look human into the realm of being unqualified.

We have all heard the horror stories of colleagues risking vulnerability with their church boards concerning struggling marriages, for example, only to be served with dismissal notices. I know of painful betrayals that have occurred when supposedly loyal followers have got close to their leader, then proceeded to use the information such closeness afforded to undermine and destabilise the leader's ministry.

It's not without reason that we tend to be guarded with our own significant and painful issues. But, these risks notwithstanding, I have come to the conclusion that the withdrawal of a leader to a supposedly safe relational distance can be more subtly destructive. By giving the entirely false impression that our lives are trouble-free by virtue of our deep spirituality, we lose our capacity to be relevant to our people. They may well be impressed by our words, but they won't feel they can be anything like us.

If we convey the idea that the end result of true spirituality is a problem-free life, then not only have we entirely misrepresented the gospel, we have also placed a burden on our people that no amount of effort on their part will remove. As spiritual as they try to be, the problems keep on coming. If they needed any proof that their spirituality wasn't up to scratch, then the daily grind of painful, intractable problems seems to provide that evidence. Instead of our lives somehow being a point of encouragement to them in their darkest hours, we appear to embody an implicit accusation. 'Pastor seems to have the victory. He's found the secret. What's wrong with me?'

Then, to make matters worse, when our clay feet begin to crumble, as inevitably happens, they find out that we weren't what we seemed. When it transpires that we battled with many of the same issues they did, and sometimes fell as badly or worse, they feel betrayed. Now our perceived hypocrisy leads to the very thing we were trying to avoid – the messenger, and thereby the message, are disrespected.

Vulnerability allows us to acknowledge, up front, that we're not perfect or problem-free. Every person's journey has good and heroic parts, and dark and cowardly episodes. There are no experts in this journey, just some who have been covered by grace for longer than others.

Patrick Lencioni, in his book *The Five Dysfunctions of a Team*, observes that trust is the most powerful trait in shaping a positive culture. 'When there is an absence of trust,' he says, 'it stems from a leader's unwillingness to be vulnerable with the group ... leaders who are not genuinely open with one another about their mistakes and weakness make it impossible to build trust.'[1]

For Karen and me, our most painful personal issue, the one that made us feel most disqualified and most vulnerable to the charge of being ineligible to continue in ministry, came in the form of a child who began by walking away from faith and ended up in a prison cell.

Dion, our firstborn, had always been a handful. As a baby, he would wake between four and seven times a night. Karen and I were utterly exhausted when Plunket (a family support organisation) stepped in. They took Karen and Dion into residential care for ten days in an attempt to curb what they thought were merely the bad habits of new parents. At the end of that time, they handed the crying baby back into our hands. The nurse shrugged her shoulders and with a weak smile said, 'He'll come right by the time he's 21.'

Dion grew to be a bright, bubbly, hyperactive child. We had never heard of Attention Deficit Disorder (ADD); I don't think anyone had in those days. Looking back, and with the benefit of a much later diagnosis, we can better appreciate what we were up against and feel somewhat relieved that it wasn't all about inadequate parenting skills – though I suspect there was some of that as well.

Dion's school reports all had a familiar ring to them: 'A delight to have in the classroom; full of fun but with a very short attention span. Dion must realise that first finished isn't always a goal to be strived for...'

Although always a challenge, Dion's primary school years were relatively uneventful. It was secondary school that began to underline his difficulties in concentration. Along with his ADD, we found he also battled with mild dyslexia. Reading was painfully difficult for him and his grades began to reflect the struggle. This took a toll on his self-esteem and, although we always tried to convince him otherwise, he became more convinced that he was, as he would put it, 'simply dumb.'

He had always been fascinated by trucks – the bigger the

better. At our church in Cambridge, we had a good friend who was a truck driver, and he began taking Dion with him on weekends and for the school holidays. Dion quickly decided that the life of a trucker was what he was born for. On leaving school, he gained his heavy trucking licence and entered the world and subculture of long hauls and big rigs.

The trucking scene is a tough world even for those hardened by long experience. The hours are exhausting and too many of the bosses notorious. Unbeknown to us, drug-taking was widespread among the drivers. For Dion, entry into the seedy underworld of narcotics came as a result of the illegal hours his employers required him to work. By keeping two log books concurrently, hiding one and then the other, they were able to keep a step ahead of law enforcement agencies, and worked hours that bordered on complete madness.

Dion began taking pills to keep himself awake, and then required other pills to bring himself down, so he could sleep during his rare breaks. The uppers and downers led to the use of speed (amphetamine). The first time we found one of the small white sachets in his bag, our naivety allowed us to believe him when he told us it belonged to a driving companion.

Church life and youth group involvement, which had been a regular part of Dion's life to this point, now dropped away almost completely. Over time, speed gave way to methamphetamines and these, in turn, led to a complete unravelling of the bright, bubbly personality we knew to be Dion. He became moody and surly. 'Hi, how was your day?' would be answered with a paranoid, 'What is this, 20 questions?' and a slammed door.

Then the dishonesty escalated. Cheques taken from the back of our cheque book were filled out for party requirements. Money taken from employers led to numerous enforced job changes. Using his excellent machine operating skills, and presenting a bright, believable personality when needed, he always managed to stay in work.

Although he had left home, we heard enough and saw enough to know Dion's path was snaking downwards towards complete breakdown. On at least two separate occasions he was able to secure our bank details and empty our accounts. Our mortgage, insurance, and all manner of other payments, bounced – to our great embarrassment and near financial ruin. The bank officials acknowledged their failures in the process. Dion had simply presented withdrawal slips to tellers who had insufficiently checked his ID details. Due to their culpability, the bank promised to return the missing money, but always on the proviso that we pressed charges against our son.

For better or worse – I'm still not sure which – and in spite of advice to the contrary from our wider family, we refused to press charges, and instead chose to absorb the losses.

In the midst of this chaos, God was unerringly faithful and often forewarned us in dreams of intense seasons of struggle ahead, or gave us scriptural promises in the midst of our current struggles and pain.

On one occasion, I was reading the Psalms early one morning and felt a portion of Psalm 20 come alive to me.

> The Lord hear thee in the day of trouble; the name of the God of Jacob defend thee; Send thee help from the

> sanctuary, and strengthen thee out of Zion; Remember all thy offerings, and accept thy burnt sacrifice; Selah (Psalm 20:1-3 KJV).

Initially the words were a great comfort, but after a week of hellish confusion brought on by being caught up in the storm of another paroxysm of drug-induced madness, I began wondering if I hadn't simply imagined that God had given me that scripture. Perhaps the whole thing had been some kind of Freudian wish fulfilment.

On the following Sunday, before heading off to church, I asked the Lord to confirm the passage to me.

'Lord could you arrange someone to come to me and give me Psalm 20 today; let it come in a prophetic word or song.'

The morning service came and went without so much as a reference to the Psalms in general, let alone Psalm 20 specifically. Nothing happened during the day that could in any way be seen as an answer to my cry. I felt a sense of anger rising, 'Lord where are you when I need you? Where are my prophetic friends? Please get one of them to call me, Lord, with Psalm 20.'

I prayed the same prayer before heading back to church for the evening service. Again nothing. As Karen and I drove home that night, a feeling of desolation seemed to overshadow me. Arriving at the house, we made our way into the kitchen and I proceeded to boil the jug for our mandatory cup of tea. Karen handed me a card and said, 'Oh, I forgot to tell you that Francie gave us a card.'

I don't want some saccharine-sweet greeting card with some

Christian-kitsch rubbish, I recall thinking, *I just wanted someone to give me Psalm 20!*

As soon as I thought the words, I immediately felt ashamed. At that moment my petulance was starkly highlighted. I stepped back several paces and apologised to the Lord for my immature peevishness.

I sat with my cup of tea and, with the best attitude I could muster, I opened and read the card that had been so generously offered. Imagine my surprise-delight-chagrin to find that, on the inside cover of the card, Francie had written out Psalm 20.

God was so amazingly faithful to us.

Some months later, Dion – as he was wont to do – simply disappeared off the radar. This was always an ominous sign to us. He refused to answer any of our calls or texts and, after a month of silence, we were anxious, to say the least. I proceeded to call all the numbers I had for his previous employers or friends, in an effort to calm the rising tide of alarm. After what seemed like incessant dead ends, I finally made contact with a couple who had shown Dion unusual kindness in a previous, particularly dark time.

'Russell, it's Don – Dion's dad. I was wondering if you had heard from him lately?'

An awkward silence followed, 'Have you not heard? Don't you know?'

My knees buckled as I slumped into the nearest chair, overwhelmed by what I can only describe as a feeling of dread.

'Know what?'

'He's in prison!'

The words resounded like a gunshot ricocheting off the

canyon walls of my heart. I sat stunned as Russell gave me the sketchy details as he understood them. Apparently unpaid fines and repeated failure to turn up to Periodic Detention had stretched judicial patience to breaking point. Dion had been arrested and sentenced to three months in prison.

That night I wrote the most difficult letter I have ever written. It wasn't so much the content of the letter that made the exercise hard. I simply told Dion of our love for him, and that our hearts and home were always, and would always, be open to him. It was addressing the letter that I found so excruciatingly painful.

As I was trying to write the prison address, my mind filled with images of Dion's early years: the curly blond hair, the hours we spent riding bikes and shooting baskets and playing cricket on the back lawn. Now prison. It wasn't meant to be like this. A sense of parental failure wasn't the major emotion in that moment; that had played a lead role earlier in Dion's wayward years, to the point of exhaustion. All I felt now was a haunting numbness.

I managed, shakily, to print the address and get the letter posted the following morning. The day after that, we received a letter from Dion – our correspondence had crossed in the mail. Dion expressed regret at the shame he felt he had caused, and reaffirmed his love for us.

Several weeks later, his sentence duly served, Dion was released. It was a very sobered young man that drove home with me that morning from the correctional facility. 'I never want to go back to that place,' he stated with determination.

In an attempt to start anew, free from past associates and

his previous, well earned, reputation, Dion moved to Australia to try his hand there.

He has, for the most part, with a few stutters, done much better and is enjoying his life in a new environment.

The point and purpose of telling the story of Dion's troubles isn't simply to give vent to what was, without doubt, the most difficult season of our lives thus far. I tell it because it highlights our vulnerability.

The only reason any of us are here is grace. We don't have to emulate Quasimodo, the Hunchback of Notre Dame, and attempt to conceal all that we imagine is unattractive about us. We can be honest about our pain and brokenness. In a beautiful irony, I have found that, rather than undermining leadership authority, vulnerability and honesty actually increase credibility and therefore authority.

Brennan Manning once commented,

> The sweet sound of amazing grace saves me from the necessity of self deception. It keeps us from denying that though Christ was victorious, the battle with lust, greed, and pride still rages within us. I can acknowledge that I am often unloving, irritable, angry and resentful with those closest to me. When I go to church I can leave my white hat at home and admit that I have failed. God not only loves me as I am, but knows me as I am. Because of this I don't need to apply any spiritual cosmetics

> to make myself presentable to Him (or others). I can accept ownership of my poverty, powerlessness and neediness.[2]

To be vulnerable is to live in grace and to be willing to acknowledge that our stories are a mixture of good, bad and indifferent. All in all, our stories are much the same as those of the people we lead.

As to the risks in being vulnerable, may I suggest that there is a difference in being vulnerable and unwisely 'spilling our guts' to all and sundry. Even Jesus only disrobed before the 12 in the upper room.

Many times, we are called to lead while in the midst of significant personal pain. Only a fool attempts to pretend that he is above pain or tries to hide it. But on the other hand, it is a wise person who knows how much to share of this pain and when to disclose it.

Vulnerability doesn't mean bleeding over all who come within 50 feet of us, but it is about being honest and open in the right settings.

One evening, I told part of the story about Dion to a group at our church. I mentioned that there had been many times when I had felt wholly inadequate and disqualified to lead.

Afterwards, several people came and explained that it was the fact that Karen and I 'walked with a limp' that actually qualified us in their eyes. We shared their pain and disillusionment; we knew the same discouragement and yet held on in hope; we were fellow 'limpers' and, in their eyes, that qualified us to lead.

CHAPTER 15

Concluding Thoughts

I recently celebrated a milestone birthday. My two-year-old granddaughter Neeve was coming to the party. On the way, she asked her mother, my daughter Janaya, how old I was.

'He's 60,' replied Janaya.

Neeve looked shocked and cast her eyes down as she uttered (I pray not prophetically), 'Oh no, he's ruined!'

Sometimes, in the early morning hours of the day, as I seek to go about my spiritual routines, I suspect she might be more right than her little mind knew!

While I'm thankful that 60 isn't the end of the road, I'm increasingly conscious that more of my lifetime lies behind me than before me.

I really don't want to end up being one of those old-timers who constantly talk about bygone days. But, at the risk of coming across in just that way, I want to conclude this book by taking a moment to reminisce.

Over the last 20 years, Karen and I have watched – sometimes with clarity and complete awe and at other times through the blurriness of a seemingly commonplace life – as God has restored Gateway from a broken and bleeding flock to a vibrant, thriving congregation.

There are moments in my morning devotions when I am simply overcome with gratitude at what God has done. I remember with a shudder those early, darker days and wonder if they really happened – they seem a lifetime ago.

Gateway is a normal church. 'Good, bad and ugly' is the way I like to describe it, with a smile, when someone asks after its health. I rejoice in that normality. It is truly the fulfilment of what once seemed like an impossible dream.

People sometimes ask, 'What is required to turn a church around? What does it take to make a dream come true?'

I have reflected on that question many times. Perhaps as a consequence of age and increasing amounts of water under the bridge, I find myself thinking about the answer with a clarity that only hindsight can afford. There are certain key things that I would say are required for a turnaround to be affected or for a dream to be fulfilled.

Apart from the elements that I have unpacked throughout the book thus far, there are a couple of other things I would like to highlight in closing.

The first will seem plainly obvious in our Christian context: a turnaround or the fulfilment of a dream requires an act of God.

Gateway's very existence is a divine miracle. By most criteria, our church should never have withstood the traumatic, seismic events of those early years. Its survival wasn't the result of individual or collective brilliance or giftedness on the part of its leader or leaders.

As I reflect on the difficult early years, as compared to the latter ones, I am keenly aware that I'm not actually doing anything significantly different now than what I did then.

I worked hard, preached to the best of my ability, prayed passionately, and watched helplessly as the tide removed more and more people from the church until we were left with a sickly shadow of the former, larger, seemingly thriving congregation.

I will never forget the lowest point in our journey. It was Mother's Day – a day in our culture on which many families give church a miss to take Mum out for brunch – and our already depleted congregation was further reduced. We had a returning missionary as our guest speaker that morning. She was a missions pioneer and had a reputation for being a straight shooter. As she got up to speak to her former home church, she surveyed the scene before her. About 300 people sat in an auditorium that could comfortably hold 1000, scattered like a sparse flock across a hillside.

'What has happened to my church?' she asked incredulously. 'Where is everybody? This is terrible. This isn't the church I knew.'

Already bruised, battered and discouraged, the remaining faithful, shoulders sunken, let out a collective sigh and probably thought of joining the exodus.

John Maxwell talks about the effects of the Law of Momentum. He says that when momentum is against you, it always makes you look worse than you really are. On the flipside, when it is flowing for you, momentum exaggerates how well you are doing.

From experience, I can testify that Maxwell makes a very shrewd observation. The Law of Momentum certainly made our leadership look shabby and inadequate in those early days.

When the turnaround began some seven years after we took the reins of leadership, I was acutely aware that it had nothing to do with any previously undiscovered key or any principle that I had recently obtained to unlock heaven's provision. There was no special book that I had read. I hadn't heard a particular message, and I hadn't attended an extraordinary conference that gave me a new power to change our fortunes. I wasn't doing anything vastly different. I continued to work hard, I kept on preaching as well as I could, and I prayed as passionately as I knew how – all in all, much the same as I had for the previous seven wilderness years. But now the results were utterly different.

The only difference was that God had stepped in to act.

In those darker moments, when we are rowing against the tide, we need to remember a vital point. God desires the turnaround, and the fulfilment of the dream that He has given us, more than we do ourselves. He has greater anticipation over it than we do.

In hindsight, I think I sometimes prayed as if I had to motivate an otherwise reluctant God. I begged Him to come into our situation and affect a transformation. The truth is, I didn't have to motivate Him. He was already motivated. What I perceived to be unwillingness on His part was actually the timing of a master strategist.

Often, God's actions simply don't fit with our timetable. We struggle with this because we have the tendency to believe that if He really cared, He would get the show up and running and on the road asap. Instead, He comes, as Galatians 4:4 states, 'In the fullness of time…' Or, as another translation has it, 'In God's strategic time…'

A comic once quipped, 'God is never late, but oh the opportunities to be early that He misses!'

Often, when Karen and I are discussing some situation that looks outwardly bleak, I find myself saying, 'All it takes is for Pharaoh to have a dream.' Joseph had no conception of how he could possibly get out of the dungeon, but God had things under control. One disturbed night of sleep and a couple of seemingly rogue dreams later, Pharaoh summons Joseph out of prison and into the royal court.

If your turnaround is going to happen, if your dream is going to be fulfilled, it needs an act of God's power. Thankfully, in His time, this is something He is very willing to provide.

A second factor in seeing a turnaround affected or a dream fulfilled is persistence on our part.

Turnarounds take time – sometimes much longer than we imagined. Patience has never been a strong suit of the flesh, and even less so in our postmodern age.

But God doesn't deal in 'microwave saints.' He is happy to take His time, and ours, to work His purposes.

I have observed that God actually uses delay as an instrument in preparing us to live successfully in the fulfilment of our dreams. As you study the lives of biblical saints, it's clear that almost every one of them knew periods of significant delay – whether it was Abraham and Sarah waiting for their promised son, Moses on the backside of the desert for 40 years, David waiting patiently for the promised Kingdom, or Paul waiting in Tarsus for his ministry to emerge.

All knew delay, and all developed persistence as they waited.

The Bible says, 'The steps of a good man are ordered by the Lord' (Psalm 37:23 KJV). I like to suggest, tongue in cheek, that the *stops* of a good man are also ordered by the Lord.

God uses delay to reveal and manifest what is truly in our hearts. In those situations, the condition of our character becomes clear.

In Exodus 32:1, Moses 'delayed to come down the mountain.' As a result, Israel turned to idolatry. The delay didn't cause the idolatry; it simply revealed the presence of idolatry in the people's hearts.

In 1 Samuel 13:8-11, Samuel delayed coming to King Saul on the battlefield. Saul, in disobedience, foolishly decided to offer the appointed sacrifice in Samuel's stead. Samuel's delay didn't cause the disobedience, it simply revealed Saul's propensity to disobey when under pressure.

God refuses to be pressured by our desire for haste. He is very secure, and is willing to be misunderstood – even maligned – for not acting with what we imagine to be the appropriate level of alacrity.

He knows what we apparently don't – that an inheritance hastily gotten at the beginning will not be blessed in the end (Proverbs 20:21).

If we are going to see God affect a turnaround and fulfill our dreams, we must develop persistence.

There's a quote, variously attributed to numerous famous people, that states,

> Nothing in the world can take the place of persistence. Talent will not. Nothing is more common than unsuccessful individuals with talent. Genius will not. Unrewarded genius is almost a proverb. Education will not. The world is full of educated derelicts. Persistence and determination alone are all powerful.

While we may not go as far as calling persistence 'all powerful', I do know that it is certainly a required element in God bringing His purposes to pass.

I suspect that many a soldier has become a hero, not because he was braver than everyone else, but simply by staying at his post for 10 minutes longer than they did.

During one difficult season of my life, I saw a particular poster in a store window. It was a picture of the cutest little kitten you could possibly imagine, hanging from a rope by one claw. It dangled hopelessly, desperately in need of rescue. The caption under the picture simply read, 'Hang in there baby.'

As I looked at the picture, it seemed that the Lord spoke those same words into my heart. At first I was shocked, thinking, 'That can't be God. He doesn't use language like that. I have never heard a prophetic word that said, "Yea, thus saith the Lord – Hang in there baby!"' But the more I thought about it, the more convinced I became that God had indeed spoken to me. He could communicate with me using whatever language He liked. Perhaps somewhat playfully, and yet ever so tenderly, He had exhorted me to persistence.

A third essential ingredient for affecting turnaround is the willingness to take personal risks. In fact, I suspect faith is actually spelt, 'R-I-S-K.'

As I think about the way things changed at Gateway, I realise how much can be attributed to the willingness – especially of our remaining congregation – to take an immense personal risk. That step involved trusting leadership again. Leaders had cruelly betrayed them. These congregation members had placed their trust, their families and finances into the hands of people who had proved unworthy of that trust. None could have blamed them for refusing to be placed in a similarly vulnerable position again.

Sometimes I try to imagine how I might have responded if I had been in Joseph's shoes when Pharaoh asked him for guidance. Joseph's experience with dream interpretation, at least up to that point, hadn't exactly been easy-going. When he shared his initial dreams with his family, he faced rejection, isolation and disapproval.

Later, when he interpreted the dreams of the butler and baker, he again faced bitter disappointment.

The butler, in the euphoria of his release from prison, failed to deliver on his promise to bring Joseph's plight to the attention of Pharaoh. Genesis 41:1 says that Joseph languished in prison for two full years. The Hebrew word for 'full' is *yowm*. In other places, this word is translated 'forever' or 'everlasting.' Those two years dragged on and on. After a week had stretched into two weeks, then weeks into months, the realisation that the butler's memory had failed him must have been a crushing blow to Joseph.

Then suddenly, Joseph is standing before one of the most powerful men in the world, being asked for another dream interpretation. It doesn't take an analytic genius to see that the trajectory associated with the interpretation of dreams had always been a downhill slide for Joseph. In the past, every time he'd used that gift, things had gone from bad to worse. I suspect my response would have been to politely explain to Pharaoh that I no longer possessed the gift of dream interpretation.

But Joseph takes a risk.

He interprets Pharaoh's dreams. It was his willingness to take that chance, and the subsequent wisdom he exhibited, that catapulted Joseph out of the dungeon and into a role as Pharaoh's right-hand man.

An assessment of people who have gained the fulfilment of their dreams shows that it is par for the course for them to embrace situations which, for all the world, look like nothing more than places of hurt and difficulty.

The faithful people who remained after the traumatic events of failed leadership at Gateway took that risk. Karen and I will be forever in their debt. Without their willingness to trust us and the leadership team that grew around us, there would have been no Gateway to lead.

I really struggled with a title for this book. Nothing seemed to gel. Somewhere in the process, the old adage, 'water under the bridge,' popped into my head.

Certainly a lot of water has flowed under Gateway's 'bridge' over the past 20 years or so. In a moment of unguarded cynicism, I couldn't help feeling that it hadn't only been water – there had been a load of other 'stuff' too. Out of that thought, the title took shape.

In the early days, there seemed at times to be more stuff than water, and I sometimes wondered if the polluted stream would ever run clean again. It has, and for that – and to the One who has done the cleaning – I am, and will remain, eternally grateful.

That thought, along with all the other ideas that I've covered in this book, is the encouragement I'd like to leave with you. You can take it from me that God is always faithful, even in the most difficult times. He wants to see you grow as a leader in and through it all, and His love will propel you forward to the day when, you too, can observe the water under the bridge and see how far He has brought you.

Notes

Introduction

1. Frederick Buechner. *Now and Then: A Memoir of Vocation.* Harper San Francisco 1991 Reprint Edition. Page 2.
2. Ibid. Page 2.

Chapter One – Gathering Clouds

1. Jon Krakauer. *Into Thin Air*. Macmillan Main Market Ed. 1999.
2. C S Lewis. *The Four Loves*. Mariner Books 1971. Page 49.

Chapter Two – The Storm Breaks

1. J R R Tolkien. *The Lord of the Rings – Fellowship of the Ring*. Unwin paperbacks 1979. Page 78.

Chapter Three – What Was All That About?

1. R Paul Stevens. *Down to Earth Spirituality*. IVP Books. 2004. Page 84.
2. Gene Edwards. *Tale of Three Kings*. Tyndale House Publishers. 1980.
3. Dan Allender. *Leading with a Limp*. Waterbrook Press. 2006. Page 96.
4. Richard Foster. *Celebration of Discipline*. Hodder & Stoughton 1980. Page 110.

5. E Stanley Jones. *In Christ*. Abingdon Press. 1961. Page 95.
6. Langdon Gilkey. *Shantung Compound: The Story of Men and Women Under Pressure*. HarperCollins Publishers. 1966. Page 66-67.
7. G W F Hegel. *Philosophy of Right*. 1820. Dove Publications 2005.

Chapter Four – The Vision Thing

1. Jim Collins. *Good to Great*. Harper Business 2001. Page 45.
2. Leonard Sweet. *Nudge: Awakening Each Other to the God Who is Already There*. David Cook. 2010. Page 207.
3. Tim Keel. *Intuitive Leadership*. Baker Books. 2007. Page 203.
4. Ibid. Page 204.

Chapter Five – The Leader as an 'Environmental Architect'

1. Samuel Chand. *Cracking your Church's Culture*. Jossey-Bass 2011. eBook 343 of 3273.
2. Ibid. 188 of 3273.
3. Edgar H Schein. *Organizational Culture of Leadership*. Jossey-Bass. 4th Edition. 2010. eBook 199 of 8142.
4. Lyle Schaller. *Getting Things Done*. Abingdon Press. 1987. Used by permission of Abingdon Press, all rights received.
5. Max De Pree. Copyright © 1989. First appeared in *Leadership is an Art* published by Doubleday. Used with permission of the author and Sandra Dijkstra Literary Agency.
6. Oz Guinness. *The Call*. Thomas Nelson. 2003. Page 137.
7. Edgar H Schein. *Organizational Culture of Leadership*. Jossey-Bass. 4th Edition. 2010.
8. E M Bounds. *Power Through Prayer*. Trinity Press. 2012. Page 39.

9. Frederick Buechner. *Alphabet of Grace*. Harper One. Reprint Edition. 2009. Page 114.
10. Edgar H Schein. *Organizational Culture and Leadership*. Jossey-Bass. 4th Edition. 2010. Page 247.
11. Steven Kerr. 'On the Folly of Rewarding A while Hoping for B.' *Academy of Management Executive*. Vol. 9. No. 1. 1995.
12. Leonard Sweet. *Viral: How Social Networking is Poised to Ignite Revival*. Waterbrook Press 2012. Page 108.
13. Daniel A Brown. *The Other Side of Pastoral Ministry: Using Process Leadership to Transform your Church*. Commended to the Word. 2014.
14. Edgar H Schein. *Organizational Culture and Leadership*. Jossey-Bass. 4th Edition. 2010. Page 257.

Chapter Six – Valuing People

1. Brennan Manning. *The Ragamuffin Gospel*. Multnomah Publishers. 1900, 2000. Page 134.
2. Eugene Kennedy. *The Choice to be Human: Jesus Alive in the Gospel of Matthew*. Doubleday. 1985. Page 8.
3. Brennan Manning. *The Signature of Jesus*. Multnomah Publishers. 1996. Page 106.
4. C S Lewis. *God in the Dock: Essays on Theology and Ethics*. W M B Eerdman's Publishing Co. 1972.

Chapter Eight – Sexual Failure in Ministry

1. Robert Clinton. Article, 'Finishing Well: Six Characteristics'. 2007.
2. Peter Rutter. *Sex in the Forbidden Zone*. HarperCollins Publishers. 1990.
3. Margaret Evening. *Who Walk Alone*. IVP. 1974.

4. Dean Ludwig & Clinton Longenecker. 'The Bathsheba Syndrome.' *Journal of Business Ethics*. 1993. Pages 265-273.

Chapter Eleven – The Value of Integrity

1. Andrew Lloyd Webber & Timothy Rice. *Jesus Christ Superstar*. Song: 'Judas' Death.' Used with permission.

Chapter Twelve – More Nasty Surprises

1. Warren Bennis. *Why Leaders Can't Lead*. Jossey-Bass. 1989.

Chapter Thirteen – Finding Our Redemptive Fingerprint

1. *Newsweek*, 'What Lies Behind the Huge Cultural Shift in Thinking About Plastic Surgery.' May 27th. 1985.

Chapter Fourteen – The Value of Vulnerability

1. Patrick Lencioni. *The Five Dysfunctions of a Team*. Jossey-Bass. 1st Edition. 2002. Page 188.
2. Brennan Manning. *The Ragamuffin Gospel*. Multnomah Publishing Inc. 1990. Page 25.

All quotations used by permission.

Bible Permissions

About the Author

Don Barry has been involved in church leadership for over 40 years. For the last 20 years he and his wife Karen have been the senior leaders of Gateway Church in Hamilton, New Zealand. During this season they have watched as God has restored a church, broken and bruised by the sexual failure of leadership, into a thriving congregation of over 1200 people. Don is a gifted teacher whose ministry has been appreciated throughout New Zealand and in many other nations. Don and Karen have been married for 42 years and have two adult children and four precious grandchildren.

Printed in Great Britain
by Amazon

75515676R00119